P9-BZB-641

BACK THEN

1

BACK THEN:
A PICTORIAL HISTORY OF AMERICA'S NATIONAL PARKS

Special thanks to the United States Library of Congress, whose vast pictorial archives made this book possible.

Copyright©1990 NorthWord Press, Inc.

All rights reserved. No part of this work covered by the copyrights hereon may be reproduced or used in any form or by any means — graphic, electronic or mechanical, including photocopying, recording, taping or information storage and retrieval systems — without the prior written permission of the publisher.

NorthWord Press, Inc.
Box 1360
Minocqua, WI 54548

For a free catalog describing NorthWord's line of nature and pictorial history books and gifts, call 1-800-336-5666

ISBN 1-55971-075-6

To the people who years ago got me started in the national parks—S. Herbert Evison, Ronald F. Lee, Conrad L. Wirth, Sam P. Weems and, a little later, Horace M. Albright—And to my friends inside and outside of the National Park Service who keep me going.

TABLE OF CONTENTS

BACK THEN IN THE NATIONAL PARKS

Michael Frome

DISCOVERING THE TREASURES

I treasure my books on the early days of the national parks, especially those written by the people who helped shape the parks as we know them now. At hand I have *Our National Parks* the pioneering guidebook by John Muir which first appeared in 1901. My copy is a reprint edition of 1981, but I do have an original edition of *Your National Parks*, by Enos A. Mills, published in 1917, and, even more valuable, an original of *The National Parks Portfolio*, by Robert Sterling Yard, published by the National Park Service in 1916, the very year the agency was established, as well as a subsequent edition of 1931. I also have an original of *Tales of a Pathfinder*, by A.L. Westgard, published in 1920, a summation of the author's adventures inspecting, mapping and writing about the delights of the open road and the life of the great outdoors.

Westgard was a national parks enthusiast. He wanted every American, worthy of the name, to visit these precious places before venturing elsewhere in the world. There are no glaciers in the Alps, he wrote, surpassing those of Glacier National Park; no geysers anywhere approaching in interest those of Yellowstone National Park; no chasm faintly approaching the indescribable colors and vastness of the Grand Canyon. He described Crater Lake National Park as an incomparable blue gem, and the prehistoric ruins of Mesa Verde National Park as likely ancient when the Pharaohs built the Pyramids. And where on the face of this mundane sphere, demanded Westgard, is there a spot with charms equal to those of Yosemite National Park?

Westgard lamented that national parks of his day were virtually entirely in the West, in the Rocky Mountain, Sierra Nevada and Cascade ranges. So it was in his time. But national parks as a system should reflect physical and cultural features of the entire country.

Happily, I have a copy of the 1922 edition of *Our Southern Highlanders*, by Horace Kephart, about his life in the Great Smoky Mountains. Kephart defined the glories of his environment, in words that proved instrumental in the establishment of a marvelous national park in the East. He wrote of how he loved of a morning to slip on his haversack, pick up his rifle, or maybe only a staff, and stride forth alone to enjoy the infinite variety of form and color and shade, of plant and tree and animal life, in the superb wilderness towering above the homes of men and women.

Kephart cherished the mountain people he knew in "the back of beyond." In the preface to that 1922 edition he noted the extensive changes since *Our Southern Highlanders* had first appeared nine years before. A railroad and graded highway pierced the wilderness. The great forest was falling before the loggers' crosscut saws, but there was still the chance to save most of his Eden, still unpeopled and unspoiled. The national park would accomplish that goal. President Theodore Roosevelt felt much the same about the place and purpose of national parks. John Burroughs, the popular writer on nature, called the Grand Canyon "the world's most wonderful spectacle, ever changing, alive with a million moods," but Roosevelt went further. After his first visit to the Grand Canyon in 1903, Roosevelt conveyed a strong message to the American people. "Do nothing to mar its grandeur," he pleaded. "Keep it for your children, and your children's children, and all who come after you, as the one great sight which every American should see."

In that same year, while traveling in California, he spent three days in Yosemite with John Muir. The first night they bedded down in fir boughs among giant trunks of ancient sequoias, listening to the hermit

2. *President Theodore Roosevelt and John Muir in Yosemite, 1903.*

thrush and the waterfalls tumbling down sheer cliffs. "It was like lying in a great solemn cathedral," wrote the president, "far vaster and more beautiful than any built by the hand of man." Soon after, in a speech at Stanford University, Roosevelt showed his deep interest in preserving both the coast redwoods and the giant sequoias of the Sierra Nevada:

> "I feel most emphatically that we should not turn into shingles a tree which was old when the first Egyptian conqueror penetrated to the valley of the Euphrates, which it has taken so many thousands of years to build up, and which can be put to better use. That, you may say, is not looking at the matter from the practical standpoint. There is nothing more practical than the preservation of beauty, than the preservation of anything that appeals to the higher emotions of mankind."

Reading of the past is like a treasure hunt yielding discoveries of why early-day visitors ventured to national parks even before they were national parks, and how they traveled and what they wore, of why particular areas were set aside, and of who wrote and spoke and campaigned to save them. For me, the pursuit of the national parks "back then" is sheer pleasure. For forty years I have been writing about the parks, showing people how to enjoy and yet to conserve them. I feel a concern for the future, but, as the saying goes, "How can you tell where you're going if you don't know where you've been?"

Each of the national parks has its own history, complete with pathfinders, followed by heroes and heroines who would never rest until their special places were properly protected, and chroniclers to make the wonders known and appreciated. Consider, for example, the Grand Canyon: A band of Coronado's men first saw the canyon in 1540, but it remained a legend until 1858 when it was rediscovered by an army survey party. John Wesley Powell was a professor of geology in Illinois, a one-armed veteran of the Civil War, when he first explored the Green River on a field trip in 1868. The following summer, with supplies provided by the Smithsonian Institution and the War Department, he took four small boats down the Green to the Colorado River and through the Grand Canyon, a voyage of nine hundred incredible, unknown miles, which he recounted in one of the great adventure stories of all time.

At Powell's request, Thomas Moran, the artist, came to the Grand Canyon in 1873. Two years earlier Moran had been to Yellowstone with the official survey led by Ferdinand Hayden. Once that party returned East from Yellowstone, Moran's watercolors and the photographs of William Henry Jackson were presented by Hayden at numerous congressional hearings as visible proof of Yellowstone's wonders, leading to a unanimous vote to preserve them in a national park. Now at the Grand Canyon, Moran witnessed a raging thunderstorm and made sketches for his largest and most powerful painting, *The Chasm of the Colorado*. In 1874 the painting was completed and purchased by Congress to hang in the Senate lobby opposite its companion piece, Moran's earlier masterwork, the *Grand Canyon of the Yellowstone*.

Each park has its own saga, its own memorable names. Annals of the very early days in the West include Frederick Law Olmsted at Yosemite; Cornelius Hedges, Nathaniel P. Langford and Ferdinand V. Hayden at Yellowstone; John Muir, principally at Yosemite and Sequoia, but elsewhere as well; William Gladstone Steel at Crater Lake; George Bird Grinnell at Glacier; Charles Sheldon at Mount McKinley; Enos A. Mills at Rocky Mountain. Without those individuals the parks mentioned might not exist at all today. The same holds true of parks established later and in the East: of George D. Door at Acadia; George Freeman Pollock at Shenandoah; Horace Kephart at the Great Smoky Mountains; and John D. Rockefeller, Jr., at Grand Teton.

> "Each one of these national parks in America is the result of some great man's thought of service to his fellow citizens. These parks did not just happen; they came about because earnest men and women became violently excited at the possibility of these great assets passing from public control."

So declared J. Horace McFarland in testifying before a congressional committee in 1916. McFarland, as president of the American Civic Association, did his share and more by pressing for legislation to establish a new agency to administer the parks. So the National Park Service came into being, and with it two legendary personalities: Stephen T. Mather, the first director, an energetic outdoors enthusiast and self-made millionaire who thought nothing of spending his own money for park projects when federal funding was not available; Horace M. Albright, his young assistant, and later his successor, who shared in converting an idea into a national system of natural and cultural treasures.

In the preface to the first *National Parks Portfolio*, Mather wrote that the nation possessed an empire of grandeur and beauty that was virtually unknown. "It owns the most inspiring playgrounds and the best equipped nature schools in the world," he wrote, "and is serenely ignorant of the fact." America's national parks are now known and admired the world over. The look back at history helps this generation to be proud and grateful.

Michael Frome
Huxley College of Environmental Studies June, 1990

WHEN TOURISTS CAME

High Adventure in Yosemite

Tourists discovered national parks even before the wonderlands were labeled as "parks." But first, in advance of tourists, came Indians, trappers, traders, surveyors, soldiers, and free-lance adventurers. They lived in a world of spirit as well as substance, feeling the presence of gods in sacred places and feeling sacred scenery as part of their existence. The Ahwahneechee Indians of California, for example, called their valley in the High Sierra *Ahwahnee*, "the deep grassy valley in the heart of the sky mountain." Imagery, dance, religion, health care, recreation, crafts and culture all were immediate and direct, nature-derived and nature-focused. Words that have meaning to us as place names had special, but different, meaning to them. *Yosemite* meant "full-grown grizzly bear."

The earliest sightseers included prospectors in the 1849 gold rush. They and the Indians didn't get along so the governor of California in 1851 dispatched a cadre of vigilantes called the Mariposa Battalion. The troops chased the natives out, opening the way for miners and settlers to move in. By the mid-fifties the first organized party of tourists arrived and the first hotel was built. Horace Greeley, the celebrated New York editor, came in 1859 to see how the wild Yosemite compared with great sights of the refined East, such as Niagara Falls, Natural Bridge and Mammoth Cave. Greeley was overwhelmed by massive El Capitan, Half Dome, Bridal Veil Falls, the Merced River flowing through meadows and pines, leading him to declare Yosemite Valley "the greatest marvel of the continent."

Though the valley was remote and inaccessible, tourists read such glowing reports and came. The Central Pacific Railroad in 1869 reached Stockton, a hundred miles away, but the valley was bounded by high, steep walls and the only way to enter was by horseback or muleback over rough and dangerous trails. In the mid-seventies toll roads made things a little easier, but the roads were steep and dusty. Going to Yosemite was definitely high adventure.

Once the wagon roads were built, the influx really began, with great competition among travel agencies in San Francisco, 150 miles away. Hotels were built in the valley by eager developers and entrepreneurs, while a few of Yosemite's champions considered its future and how to protect it. These stalwarts included Frederick Law Olmsted, the landscape architect who had helped design Central Park in New York City and had come to California as superintendent of General John C. Fremont's estate. The strong tide of public interest led to congressional passage in 1864 of an act granting Yosemite Valley and the Mariposa Grove of Big Trees to California as a state park to be held "inalienable for all time." Soon thereafter the governor appointed a commission, with Olmsted as chairman, to develop the land for "public use, resort and recreation." Olmsted then and thereafter saw preservation of natural scenes as beneficial to the human spirit — marking a difference between tourism in the national parks and other places tourists go.

John Muir made his first trip to Yosemite in 1868. Born in Scotland and raised in Wisconsin, he wanted nothing of cities, crowds and commerce. Though he traveled widely over the West, Muir made Yosemite his special kingdom, living in self-reliance for six years among the ice-carved peaks, immense domes and ancient forests. Muir was in great demand as a writer, but he was definitely a writer with a mission. In collaboration with Robert Underwood Johnson, editor of *Century Magazine*, Muir conducted a tireless campaign to make a national park of the Sierra peaks and slopes surrounding Yosemite Valley. They and their supporters achieved success in 1890 (and sixteen years later, in 1890, California re-ceded the valley and the Mariposa Grove to the federal government for inclusion in the park).

Why regulations came to Yellowstone

Yellowstone, meanwhile, was still an unknown wilderness when Yosemite Valley already thrived as a resort. John Colter, who left the Lewis and Clark expedition in 1806 to become a trapper and free-lance explorer, may have been the first white man to see and report on the Yellowstone country. His sober account of the wonders he beheld was received as a monumental exercise in yarn-spinning. Then Jim Bridger, rawboned, gray-eyed "Old Gabe," followed, adding his tales about the cliff of black glass, spouting hot springs, and belching sulfurous steam, which were put down as "Jim Bridger's lies." Expeditions followed, gradually building a picture of the dramatic "Yellow Rock" country.

In 1869, David E. Folsom, a local rancher, proposed designating the area as a national park. He may have been the first with the idea. The following year a significant party undertook a comprehensive reconnaissance. Led by Henry D. Washburn, surveyor general of Montana and Nathaniel Pitt Langford, with Lieutenant Gustavus C. Doane commanding a small military escort, the party covered an amazing amount of ground, mapping known wonders, discovering others, and naming sights and spectacles like Old Faithful. According to accounts, one evening around a campfire at the junction of the Firehole and Gibbon rivers, members of the group discussed what to do with the wonderland they had explored. They agreed to forego speculation with potential profit for themselves and to work for a national park — though there was no precedent for one anywhere in America or in the world. Hedges and Langford wrote articles and lectured, describing the marvels of Yellowstone and the importance of protecting them for the benefit of all the people.

Their enthusiasm led the following year to an official scientific expedition led by Ferdinand V. Hayden, director of the Geological Survey. Supported with detailed maps, plus a superb set of photographs taken by William H. Jackson and paintings by Thomas Moran, Hayden plainly showed that the scouts and trappers and the Washburn party weren't exaggerating. Congress in 1872 approved legislation of less than six hundred words setting Yellowstone apart "as a public park or pleasuring ground for the benefit and enjoyment of the people."

Visitors came, first in a mere trickle from nearby localities. But rail travel was rapidly changing America, compressing time and distance, replacing hardship with relative comfort. The Pullman car made its debut in the 1860s, the dining car in the 1880s. Roads were hacked out of the wilderness to help tourists on their way. Until the first hotel opened in 1882, however, everybody camped; those who could afford it did so in luxury, complete with guides, packers and cooks, and all the rest doing for themselves.

The narrative of one tourist of 1877, Frank Carpenter, recounts the first carefree days spent in the park by his party of nine — by day admiring the limitless wild country and geysers, followed by evenings of song and banter around the campfire. More than forty other tourists and sportsmen were roaming the park at the same time, plus more than seven hundred unexpected fellow travelers, Nez Perce Indians at war with the United States. Joseph Looking Glass, and White Bird, chiefs of the Nez Perce, were leading their people from ancestral lands further west across Canada, hoping to find safety in Canada. The Carpenter party first encountered a band of angry young warriors but were unhurt and later met Chief Joseph himself. They were impressed. 'The noble red man' we read of was more nearly impersonated in this Indian than in any I have ever met,'' wrote Carpenter's sister, Emma. "Grave and dignified, he looked a chief." The Nez Perce, alas, did not make it all the way to Canada, their epic movement ending in Montana with capture by the cavalry.

Some tourists, even then, came to Yellowstone with vandalism in mind. Armed with axes they hacked at the rims of hot springs and geysers to chip off souvenirs. They shot and bagged wild animals, driving the game into high country, and caught and wasted fish by the thousands. It was the time before regulations. Congress had established Yellowstone as a national park, the very first, but without much thought to how it should be administered. In his book *Yellowstone: A Wilderness Besieged*, historian Richard A. Bartlett comments that visitors found nature's abundance so obvious, so overwhelming, that restrictions seemed ridiculous. In due course restraint, through regulation, responsibility, and public awareness, would save the parks.

George Grinnell's Crusade

George Bird Grinnell made his first trip to Yellowstone in 1875 at the age of twenty-six while serving as a naturalist with a military party headed by Colonel William Ludlow. The previous year he had been to the Black Hills with General George Custer. Grinnell was a young New Yorker who had graduated from Yale in 1870 and declined his father's invitation to join a banking firm; instead, he headed West to live among the Plains Indians (and to write a score of books about them).

Grinnell was appalled at the wholesale and unrestrained destruction of game animals he found in Yellowstone. He became one of the leaders of the fight to prohibit the killing of wildlife in national parks. He, his friend and fellow New Yorker Theodore Roosevelt and a handful of other influential "American hunting riflemen" saw big-game species like bison and elk slaughtered in the wholesale ravishment of wild areas; they organized the Boone and Crockett Club and campaigned to keep national parks as refuges which should always be free of hunting. In 1876 Grinnell joined the staff of **Forest and Stream**, later becoming its crusading editor and publisher.

Grinnell in his youth loved horses, dogs and sporting firearms. His book, **American Duck Shooting**, is a classic in the literature of field sports. His most memorable hunt took place in the glacier country of Montana in 1885, long before it became a park. It was the first of many trips into that magnificent wilderness during which he hunted, fished, climbed mountains, explored glaciers, and luxuriated amid the scenery and wildlife.

Few white men had penetrated the mysterious country before Grinnell on that first expedition. He was accompanied by J.W. "Appekunny" Schultz, hunter, writer, and adopted member of the Blackfeet. One night they ate boiled beaver presented to them by two Indians. Then they joined forces with a band of Kootenais hunting sheep on the high slopes. In the midst of a snow squall Grinnell spotted a handsome animal and killed it with a single shot at about 150 yards. He packed out his kill over a distance of three miles, climbing 1,500 feet, then descending 2,000 feet to the nearest point accessible by horse. That night around the campfire Schultz proudly proclaimed the mountain would henceforth be known as Singleshot in honor of Grinnell's achievement.

In time, he himself conceived the names of major landmarks in the Glacier country, including Gunsight Mountain and Gunsight Pass, Swiftcurrent Mountain and Swiftcurrent Glacier. Grinnell Glacier, Grinnell Lake, and Grinnell Mountain all were named for him — and he probably regarded the establishment of Glacier National Park in 1910 as his greatest single prize.

Grinnell championed other causes. In 1886 he organized a bird protection society, which he called the Audubon Club, the first organization of its kind to carry that name; through the pages of his magazine he enrolled 50,000 members. The following year he joined in founding the Boone and Crockett Club, determined to work on issues of dwindling big game, public lands and forest resources.

One of their toughest struggles was fought to block the attempts of politically potent mining exploiters, land grabbers, market hunters, and trappers to promote a railroad through Yellowstone. In those days Cooke City and Livingston, Montana, were snakepits of poaching. Efforts of outsiders to protect the game were considered as petty interference in local affairs; provision for the railroad was very nearly enacted by Congress. But Grinnell kicked off the campaign to protect the park in 1892 by publishing a detailed brochure and distributing it to major newspapers throughout the country.

He dispatched a team of reporters to spend the winter in the park — a rugged assignment in those days. Heading the expedition was Emerson Hough, ace of the staff, accompanied by F. Jay Haynes, the pioneer photographer of Yellowstone. As luck would have it, they were on the spot to cover the arrest of Ed Howell, the notorious poacher, while he was surrounded by five freshly killed buffaloes bloating in the snow. The coverage created a national sensation, especially with the interview in which Howell admitted to Hough that he had slain eighty buffaloes, possibly one-fourth of all the wild bison left in the world.

The American people for the first time realized they owned Yellowstone and what it meant to them. The Cooke City-Livingston lobby was snowed under at last. The Lacey Act of 1894, "for the protection of Yellowstone Park," completely revamped enforcement structure and practice.

Grinnell led many crusades. His circle of friends ranged from rough frontiersmen and Indians of the tepee to scholars, statesmen and presidents. When Calvin Coolidge in 1925 presented him with the Roosevelt Memorial Medal, the president told Grinnell: "Few men have done as much as you, and none has done more, to preserve vast areas of picturesque wilderness for the eyes of posterity in the simple majesty in which you and your fellow pioneers first beheld them."

Life ended for the pioneer conservation editor in 1938 in his eighty-ninth year. He was modest by nature and cared little for self-glorification. His memorial is in Glacier National Park, where a thousand waterfalls tumble from glacial snow masses into sparkling lakes and streams surrounded by primeval forests. Before the turn of the century, grizzlies were trapped in the glacier country for their furry hides; elk, moose, sheep, goats and deer were slaughtered so their carcasses could be used for bear bait. Establishment of the park in 1910 provided sanctuary for these species, as well as the mountain lion, coyote, lynx, hawk, and eagle. Grinnell would be proud.

Heyday of the railroads

Louis W. Hill, president of the Great Northern Railroad, became a powerful ally of George Bird Grinnell in the campaign to establish Glacier National Park. "Every passenger that goes to the national parks, wherever he may be," Hill once said, "represents practically a net earning." That was the common feeling about railroad people: Parks were good for business; they deserved support.

In the years after the Civil War the railroads had already opened the continent and changed the way Americans looked at it. People could get around and go places, and they didn't necessarily have to be rich. Even the rich changed; instead of going to traditional watering places like Saratoga in New York or Hot Springs in Virginia with a huge wardrobe for an entire season, they could explore the Golden West — with their own private railroad cars, if they were rich enough.

The change didn't come overnight, but once started there was no stopping it. In 1872, Yellowstone was still six hundred miles from the trailhead of the Northern Pacific Railroad. Eleven years later, however, the first big hotel in the park, at Mammoth Hot Springs, was opened by financial interests allied with the Northern Pacific. By the 1890s the Grand Canyon and Yosemite, as well as Yellowstone, were strong destinations for tours of the West by rail.

Railroads were a strong presence in the parks. Soon after the turn of the century the Santa Fe provided visitor accommodations at the south rim of the Grand Canyon with the beautiful El Tovar Hotel. The Union Pacific followed with accommodations at Zion, Bryce, and the north rim of the Grand Canyon and the Chicago, Milwaukee & St. Paul at Mount Rainier. The Great Northern would hardly be outdone, building Lake McDonald Lodge, "the showpiece of the northern Rockies," and a network of chalets at Glacier. The railroad tradition prevailed. At the Grand Canyon, the Fred Harvey Company assumed operations of El Tovar and Bright Angel Lodge, as well as Phantom Ranch at the bottom of the canyon. It was fitting, considering that Fred Harvey had opened his first restaurant at the Santa Fe depot in Topeka in 1876, before there were dining cars and when trains stopped along the way to feed their passengers. That was the first of the popular Harvey Houses, staffed by the celebrated smiling Harvey girls.

The railroads consciously boosted tourism. The Southern Pacific started *Sunset* magazine as part of its tourism promotion (then later gave it up). The railroads rallied behind the slogan "See America First," which to a large degree meant "See the National Parks." In 1915 the Santa Fe and Union Pacific spent half a million dollars at the San Francisco Panama-Pacific Exposition on national parks exhibits, including a scale replica of Old Faithful Inn and a make-believe Old Faithful erupting every hour just like the original. And the next year seventeen railroads contributed $43,000 to finance the first edition of the *National Parks Portfolio*, the beautiful booklet prepared by Robert Sterling Yard.

The railroads packaged the parks with all-inclusive rates covering lodging, food, and sightseeing as well as transportation. The idea of ordinary citizens going to the wild west was pretty heady stuff in 1919. H.V. Kaltenborn, then an enterprising editor of the *Brooklyn*

Eagle (and later a network radio commentator), conducted a series of national park tours that made front-page news in the *Eagle* and received considerable coverage elsewhere. The first tour, taken by 130 people, called Eaglets, lasted a month and visited four national parks — Rocky Mountain, Yellowstone, Glacier and Mount Rainier. Thirty of the Eaglets left the train at Denver to travel "the Incomparable Circle" for by bus 1,670 miles to Glacier. At Glacier the Blackfeet Indians congenially put on war paint, danced, and inducted Kaltenborn into the tribe, giving him the name Chief Fish Wolf Robe.

Rail travel opened the parks but in turn yielded to another mode of transportation. In 1914 A.L. Westgard, the highway pathfinder, visited the Grand Canyon in a motor car for the first time. Only an occasional local car from Flagstaff and one or two from long distance had ever been there. There was no garage, no fuel service. Westgard persuaded the El Tovar manager to keep his car overnight in the carriage barn. But when he recommended installing a garage, since, he said, more motorists were sure to follow, the manager replied that he didn't care for that kind of patronage and, in any case, few motorists would brave the wilds of Arizona. Two years later Westgard returned to find a large, well- equipped garage which that summer had housed over twelve hundred cars, and a large extension was already under construction.

Better wear britches than bloomers

What did tourists wear in the days back then? Since the parks were mostly in high mountain country, it was best to bring warm clothing suitable for rough outdoor use. Woolen trousers or riding breeches and woolen underwear were desirable, not only because of their warmth but for protection in rainy weather. Women who expected to climb would do well with riding breeches, as bloomers might get caught on bushes and offer too much resistance to the wind. Likewise, a flannel middy blouse would allow free use of the arms and body and be far superior to the shirt waist.

A felt hat was best for both men and women; it could be pulled down over the eyes as protection from the sun and would be far superior to a cap during a rainstorm. Heavy, comfortable shoes and woolen socks or stockings were essential for those going to tramp. Wet shoes could be worn so long as the socks were dry; the shoes might feel cold and clammy at first, but brisk tramping would soon make the feet warm and comfortable.

In *Camping and Woodcraft*, by Horace Kephart, "the bible of the outdoors," first published in 1906, the traveler was urged to plan and prepare at least six months in advance. One could start by collecting outfitters' catalogues, comparing one with another before making purchases; it would help to avoid falling prey to the plausible clerk and enable the traveler to make a selection stamped with his own individuality. Better yet would be to make things for oneself, for a ready-made camping outfit was certain to be loaded with useless gimcracks and to lack something absolutely critical.

So the thing to do on long winter evenings was to sort over the beloved duffel, to make and fit up the little boxes and hold-alls in which everything had its proper place, to fish around for materials in odd corners, and to flog one's wits with the same old problem of how to save weight and bulk without sacrificing utility. A camper should know for himself how to outfit — plus, how to select and make a camp, how to wield an axe and make proper fires, how to cook, wash, mend how to travel without losing course, or what to do when he has lost it. Such an individual, in Kephart's book, could take honest pride in resourcefulness, a sense of reserve force, self-reliance that is good to feel.

The lake is still "Majesty"

William Gladstone Steel saw Crater Lake for the first time in 1885. The lake before then was known to the Indians and a few prospectors, but it was remote, in the wild Oregon Cascades, and scarcely visited. Steel, however, was overwhelmed by the blueness of the water and the beauty of the setting, cradled in the basin of the vanished volcano, rising a thousand feet above the waterline. While standing at the rim, he committed himself to making it a national park. From then on Steel devoted his life, and his money, to this cause. He began with a petition to President Grover Cleveland that all lands around Crater Lake be withdrawn from homesteading and other claims. This was granted in 1886.

Steel worked tirelessly, building support and scientific data and influencing Oregon's congressional delegation until the park was established in 1902. Within three years a passable road was completed to the crater. A home and office were built for the park superintendent. A total of 1,500 campers came in a single year. They could camp anywhere and do whatever they pleased, considering the park had only one ranger, two at the most. When the ranger left the park at the end of September, poachers and vandals moved in, roaming around on snowshoes.

Steel did everything he could to gain recognition for the park. In 1907 he was given a permit to operate campgrounds, transportation, and boats on Crater Lake. The number of visitors rose steadily but the park was remote and received little official attention. At the 1911 national parks conference he said: "Aside from the United States government itself, every penny that was ever spent in the creation of Crater Lake National Park came out of my pocket and, besides that, it required many years of hard labor that was freely given... All the money I have is in the park, and if I had more it would go there too." It was Steel's life's work. From 1913 to 1916 he worked as superintendent of the park. Unfortunately, when Stephen T. Mather, the first director of the National Park Service, came to inspect, he was not much impressed. He thought the roads looked like animal trails, the visitor services were grossly inadequate, and nature had done more for the park than pioneers like Steel.

But that was 1916. Mather might feel otherwise today. Hiking to the rim at daybreak, a visitor finds the water calm and mirror-like, affording a reflection of the peaks above it. It is possible to have the landscape to oneself, at least at this early hour. Crater Lake once was called "Lake Majesty," a name that would still be fitting today. In contrast to other great American lakes, like Lake Tahoe, that fall in the category of paradise lost, Crater Lake retains much of its original wilderness character, not solely in its deep blue water but also in the surrounding environment of green meadows, forests, canyons, streams, and pumice desert flats. The legacy is nature unspoiled, as Mather noted, but the bequest comes from William Gladstone Steel.

Alone in Denali, every day a fresh adventure

Charles Sheldon got his first look at Denali in 1906. Towering above lesser peaks around it, the majestic dome dominated the landscape. Sheldon had seen many other mountains in Alaska and elsewhere, but they seemed almost insignificant compared with the stupendous immensity before his eyes. He camped with his two guides and helpers far above timberline and during the course of the trip observed to one of them, Harry Karstens, that the area would make a fine park and game preserve.

Sheldon was thirty-nine at the time, a civil engineer who had made successful mining and railroad investments in Mexico, and had become fascinated by desert bighorn sheep. In fact, three years earlier, at the age of thirty-six, he had retired from business to explore and study wild sheep of North America, from Mexico to Arizona and north to the Canadian Rockies and Alaska.

Denali, in central Alaska, was still wild and unexplored. The first ripples of civilization had only reached the mountain with the great gold rush of the 1890s. The native peoples knew it as Denali, the High One; the early Russians called it **Bolshaya Gora**, Big Mountain. But William A. Dickey, a young Easterner, was a member of a party that approached the base in 1896 and gave it the American name **McKinley**. Dickey, in an enthusiastic account in the **New York Sun** following his return home, explained he had named it after William McKinley of Ohio, whose nomination for the presidency was "the first news we received on our way out of that wonderful wilderness."

For his part, Sheldon was so taken with Denali that he returned in 1907 and 1908. With the help of three packers, he built a cabin on a bar of the Toklat River in the shadow of Denali's twin peaks, 20,320 feet and 19,470 feet, rising 17,000 feet above the plain, and above its massive neighbors, Foraker, Silverthrone, Crosson, Mather, and Russell, all covered with snow and huge active glaciers. Sheldon was even more impressed with the abundance and variety of wildlife. He hunted for food, collected and prepared specimens for the Smithsonian Institution, and kept detailed notes for his classic book, **The Wilderness of Denali**. He lived mostly alone, though his guide, Harry Karstens, made trips by dogsled to take

specimens for shipment and return with supplies. In a single day Sheldon saw bears, moose, more than five hundred mountain sheep, and caribou numbering in the thousands. "No words can describe my sorrow and regret," he wrote on leaving the region in June 1908, "as I led the horse out of the woods from the cabin to the bar and started down the river."

Growth and change around Denali during ensuing years concerned Sheldon. In 1909 he addressed the annual dinner of the Boone and Crockett Club, the club originally founded by Theodore Roosevelt, and enlisted its active support in his campaign for a national park. When the federal government in 1915 began construction of the Alaska Railroad, with the right-of-way skirting the proposed park border, the campaign shifted into high gear. It was strongly supported by Stephen T. Mather, the dynamic businessman who had just come to Washington to assume charge of the national parks. Sheldon, Mather and their allies rejoiced when early in 1917 Congress voted to establish the new park. In a ceremony at the White House, President Woodrow Wilson signed the park bill into law, then turned to Charles Sheldon, standing at hand, and presented him with the pen.

Harry Karstens became the first park superintendent, starting his administration with a simple wooden hut. In 1924 a total of sixty-two visitors was recorded. a camp was established that year on the Savage River for twenty-four visitors. Today, in contrast, the national park is the major tourist attraction of Alaska, the annual number of visitors totaling more than 400,000.

Sheldon envisioned Denali as a perpetual sanctuary for wildlife. So did Adolph Murie, who, starting in the early 1920s, spent a total of twenty-five summers, and some winters, pursuing wildlife research in the park. He spent long hours observing grizzly bears, often following a bear family for several days; he could distinguish different bear families, even the mothers and cubs. He saw the national park idea as a far-reaching cultural achievement, with values of the human heart and spirit taking precedence.

There is much to learn in the high-speed, high-tech present from the past, when the traveler needed time and patience to make an experience memorable. To Murie, as to Sheldon, every day in the park was a fresh adventure: catching sight of a wolf or wolverine, moving slowly and stopping occasionally to examine the landscape for animal life — the mountains for Dall sheep, river bars and passes for grizzlies and caribou, and the water for birds, beaver, and moose.

Rocky Mountains scenery of the sky

As a young man, Enos A. Mills met John Muir in San Francisco and felt inspired, recording later that he owed everything to Muir and might otherwise have turned into a gypsy. Following their encounter Mills went to Colorado, built a cabin and then an inn at the foot of towering Long's Peak, assuming his chosen role as "John Muir of the Rockies."

In 1909, Mills began his crusade for a national park in the untamed portion of the Front Range, which der-

ives its name from being the first wave of the Rockies to rise from the central Great Plains. Settlers had arrived in this region with the 1859 Colorado Gold Rush and then again in 1872 with the Irish nobleman, the Earl of Dunraven. The earl fell in love with the country and proceeded to develop a great estate and game preserve, saving many beauty spots from being picked over by prospectors. He entertained Albert Bierstadt, the German-born painter of classic Rocky Mountain landscapes, who captured on canvas the glory of many of the area's magnificent scenes.

Mills wrote and spoke extensively on the wonders of the Rockies — the brilliant colored aspen contrasting with pines and blue spruce in sheltered valleys; peaks, long ridges, and high alpine tundra; and high summits mantled in perpetual snow. First he succeeded in convincing the Colorado legislature to memorialize Congress for establishment of the new park. But most of the land involved already was administered by the U.S. Forest Service, which opposed the proposal. Mills persisted and in 1915 Rocky Mountain National Park was established. At the ceremony dedicating the park, an event which Mills also organized and supervised, notables and nature enthusiasts were abundant. The event, according to the **Rocky Mountain News**, inspired a rendition of the national anthem 'probably never given by so many voices at so high an altitude before.''

Two years later, in 1917, Mills published his guidebook, **Your National Parks.** He covered all seventeen parks established by that time, urging addition of at least twenty others. ''Thus protected,'' he wrote, ''these wildernesses will remain forever wild, forever mysterious and primeval, holding for the visitor the spell of the outdoors, exciting the spirit of exploration.'' As for his beloved Rockies: ''These snowy, rugged-tops give one a thrill as they appear to join with the clouds, and form a horizon that seems to be a part of the scenery of the sky.'' Mills reserved in his guidebook a special chapter of tribute to his model, John Muir, who had died less than three years before, and whose memory, he wrote, would always be associated with the national parks and with nature's songs in wild gardens of the world.

Snakes in the Skyland dining room

George Freeman Pollock grew up in Washington, D.C., but even as a young boy yearned to develop skills as a naturalist and explore the mountains — not the mountains of the West, but those in the Blue Ridge of Virginia, which in the late nineteenth century seemed as far removed and as wild, though only seventy miles southwest of the national capital. In 1894, when he was twenty-five, Pollock headed for the hills, setting up Stony Man Camp, a cluster of tents, and invited paying guests. In time he built log cottages and called his resort Skyland.

He was a colorful personality, who learned to deal with mountain people as a friend. The local people were real southern mountaineers living in remote isolation: loggers, shingle makers, and subsistence farmers grazing cattle, sheep and hogs, and collecting tanbark and chestnuts

for food and barter. Pollock proved to them that he was a crack shot who could make his way in the mountains as well as anyone.

He led his guests where there were no trails. A trim, dapper figure in white riding breeches, he would be on horseback at 7 a.m., blowing the bugle to get everybody out. And off they would go, with Pollock's pet Pomeranian perched on his saddle. He fed his guests well, each week, heading for the market and returning with lobster, shrimp and oysters. But he also kept a bathtub full of snakes and would often bring one or more into the dining hall. Like a mountaineer showman, Pollock enjoyed putting on snake shows. ''I would pick up good-sized rattlers in my mouth,'' he wrote later, ''as do the Hopi Indians who perform the famous snake dances in Arizona; and during the last year before ceasing to handle snakes, I even found that I could control rattlers' nervousness to such an extent that, on command, they would either begin to rattle or stop rattling.'' But he found more pleasure in the performances than did his guests, and finally he quit.

There was still plenty to do. He loved the Appalachians and wanted the Skyline ridge protected in a national park, like the great parks in the West. As early as 1907 he found a friend and ally in young Harry Flood Byrd (the brother of Richard E. Byrd), who came to Skyland with his father. The only way to reach the resort in those days was by horseback or buckboard, but the elder Byrd owned a cottage at Skyland which he gave to Harry as a wedding present, starting with his honeymoon. Byrd was a self-avowed mountain lover and for years to come, even while serving as governor of Virginia and United States Senator, would keep coming back. He climbed every peak in the mountains and his favorite, Old Rag, every year.

In 1924 Pollock felt challenged when the Secretary of the Interior appointed a Southern Appalachian National Park Commission to identify the choice site for a new national park. At first, attention focused on the Massanutten Mountains, a great ridge fifty miles long, but Pollock invited the members of the commission to Skyland to inspect the Blue Ridge. Ultimately they were convinced, ''It will surprise the American people,'' the commission reported, ''that a national park site within a three-hour ride of our National Capital and within a day's ride of 40,000,000 of our inhabitants. It has many canyons and gorges, with beautiful cascading streams. It has some primeval forests, and the opportunity is there to develop an animal refuge of national importance.''

When the park was authorized in 1926, every acre was in private ownership. It was up to the state of Virginia to acquire the land for presentation to the federal government. Governor Harry F. Byrd played a key role in recommending the appropriation of funds by the state legislature. ''In the tragedies and other strain of our modern world,'' he would write years later, ''generations to come will receive peace of mind and new hopes in lifting their eyes to the peaks and canyons of the Shenandoah National Park and those who made possible its establishment can justly feel that their labors were not in vain.''

The prime mover was George Freeman Pollock, who championed the treasures of the mountains but wanted to share them as well. In 1928, when getting to Skyland was still an arduous endeavor he welcomed the first trip of the Potomac Appalachian Trail. The club members placed directional signs on trails that Pollock had laid out,

then ran yearly trips to Skyland and held conferences there.

In 1937 Pollock sold Skyland. He died in Takoma Park, Maryland, in 1949, a few weeks before his eightieth birthday. Two years later Pollock Knob was dedicated in his honor. His old friend Harry F. Byrd, principal speaker for the occasion, declared that naming this prominent feature for ''the Father of Shenandoah National Park'' was an act of ''simple justice to a great American character.''

PARK PEOPLE

Yellowstone, in 1872, became the first national park. It was the only one until 1890, when three new parks — Sequoia, General Grant (later to be enlarged and renamed Kings Canyon) and Yosemite, all in California — were established. In the last decade of the nineteenth century and first decade of the twentieth others were added, including Mount Rainier, Crater Lake, Rocky Mountain, Mesa Verde, and Hawaii. These are the oldest of our national parks.

Mesa Verde, the ''green tableland'' near the Four Corners in southwest Colorado, was not set aside as a natural scenic wonder, like the other parks, but rather as one of the magnificent cliff dwellings, pueblo ruins and early missions of the Southwest subject to plunder by predatory pot hunters and vandals. In addition to establishing Mesa Verde, Congress in the same year, 1906, adopted the Antiquities Act, authorizing the president to proclaim as national monuments singular historic landmarks, historic and prehistoric structures ''and other objects of historic interest'' situated on federal lands. President Theodore Roosevelt presently proclaimed as the first national monument Devils Tower, a massive stone pillar in Wyoming that had long served as a guidepost for Indians, explorers, and settlers.

Other areas were added, but always individually, without thought as to who would run them, and with scant funding. Yellowstone in its early days was virtually at the mercy of neighbors who poached and slaughtered game whenever they chose. Luckily, in 1886, the U.S. Army took over and for the next thirty years administered Yellowstone, and other parks as well.

From all accounts, the military provided effective control at a critical time. But preserving natural and cultural resources was not its mission. Something new was needed, a central administration, a system providing direction for existing national parks and the expected new parks. Horace McFarland, of Pennsylvania, president of the American Civic Association, complained that, ''Nowhere in official Washington can an inquirer find an office of the national parks or a single desk devoted solely to their management.'' Thus, in 1915, Stephen T. Mather, a Californian, outdoorsman and self-made millionaire, arrived in Washington to take over. The story is told that Mather wrote a letter of complaint about

deplorable conditions in the parks to his old college friend Franklin K. Lane, now the Secretary of the Interior, whereupon Lane invited Mather to come aboard and show how it should be done.

In 1916 Congress voted to establish a new bureau, the National Park Service. The entire Washington staff consisted at first of three persons. One was a secretary-stenographer, whose name has been forgotten. The other two were Mather and his assistant, Horace M. Albright, a bright young Californian, his close associate and friend. The three of them were tucked away in a tiny office, and out of the mainstream of affairs.

Mather, however, was a go-getter, a born promoter. He traveled in the field in his big Packard touring car (license US NPS-1), proudly wearing his Park Service uniform; he cultivated the railroads and their political power and personally conducted the foremost editors of the day on show-me trips. Where funds were not available he spent his own. For example, he hired Robert Sterling Yard, the gifted writer and editor, first for the government and then as executive director of the National Parks Association, with a mission of involving the public in national park affairs.

Mather was determined to build a field force of professional rangers as a model of honorable and ethical federal employment. He refused to hire park superintendents based on patronage, insisting he would set the standards based strictly on merit and pick his own people. In Mather's day operating funds were meager and promotions were rare, but he inspired the National Park Service ''mystique,'' a spirit of mission, a willingness to stand tough against what he called ''desecration of the people's playground for the benefit of a few individuals or corporations.'' As Mather summed it up in a challenge for public support:

> ''Is there not some place in this great nation of ours where lakes can be preserved in their natural state; where we and all generations to follow us can enjoy the beauty and charm of mountain waters in the midst of primeval forests?''

Albright, meanwhile, divided his time between Washington and the field. He spent part of each year as superintendent of Yellowstone, where he was known as the "Duke of Yellowstone" for his entertaining of princes and presidents. But he was also a field man determined to know every bit of the vast park as well as any ranger; thus, in the fall of 1920 Albright undertook a two-hundred-mile pack trip into the wild southwest corner of the park. A ranger, he wrote in defining criteria for applicants, must be tactful, diplomatic, and courteous, with outdoors experience in riding, camping, woodcraft, and fighting fires. The pay was only $100 per month, and the ranger had to pay for his own meals, buy his own uniform, and "bring his own bed." Many brought their own horses as well. Albright made it clear there would be no soft and easy jobs in the National Park Service. "The ranger's job is especially hard," he advised the applicants. "Apply if you are qualified. Otherwise, please plan to visit the Yellowstone National Park as a tourist."

In 1924 John D. Rockefeller Jr. contacted Director Mather, though he didn't know him personally, asking for aid in planning a tour of the western parks with his three oldest sons, John, Laurance and Nelson. Rockefeller, as a preeminent philanthropist, already had some association with national parks, principally with Acadia in Maine. He had been among the elite Bar Harbor summer residents responding to George B. Dorr's appeal to preserve Mount Desert Island, leading to the establishment of Sieur de Mont National Monument in 1916 (later to be Acadia National Park). Mather instructed the superintendents to make themselves available, but to restrain themselves from talking about park needs unless specifically asked. Albright, as superintendent of Yellowstone, prepared himself.

At the moment of their meeting at the rail depot in Gardiner, Montana (as he recalled later), John III, eighteen, was recording in a notebook the amounts paid in tips to Pullman porters; Nelson, the future governor of New York and also destined to become Vice President, then sixteen, was engaged in helping porters transfer baggage from the train to Yellowstone Park buses for a group of tourists. That meeting was the beginning of a long and close relationship between Albright and the elder Rockefeller.

In 1929, Albright succeeded his mentor, Steve Mather, and served as director of the National Park Service for four fruitful years. He left to enter private business but spent much of his time as advisor on conservation affairs to John D. Rockefeller, Jr., and his son Laurance. Based on his counsel, they made contributions enabling the acquisition of land required for the establishment of three great national parks — Great Smoky Mountains, Grand Tetons, and Virgin Islands — plus funding for many other park projects. "I do not believe they could have been done at all," Albright once wrote, "without the basic compulsion to save what we prize for our fellows and for our children."

On a beautiful sunshiny day in August 1919, Heine Loss, a highly competent wrangler, and young Herbert Evison waited at the railroad station in Fairfax, Washington, with Loss' string of pack and saddle animals. Fairfax was a "coal-and-coke" village with a row of beehive ovens that filled the air with noxious gases; it was also the entry point by highway and rail to the northwestern quarter of Mount Rainier National Park.

They were waiting to meet and join a party of notables, including Stephen T. Mather, director of the new National Park Service, to spend several days on horseback in the park. The five official members of the party arrived at the station by car after driving from Paradise Valley on the opposite side of the mountain. Besides Mather the party included David Whitcomb, a prominent Tacoma businessman, president of the Rainier National Park Company, the concession firm that had built Paradise Inn, the picturesque and handsome hotel in Paradise Valley; Everett Griggs, a Tacoma lumberman and member of the park company board; Roger W. Toll, a famed mountain climber who was then superintendent of the national park, and a park ranger named Curtis.

"Herbert, what are you doing here?" asked Whitcomb in surprise. Evison was one of his employees, a secretary, for only a month after coming home from the Army. He was, Evison explained, the party's self-appointed cook, eager to play a part in this historic trip. Whitcomb accepted the explanation and the party headed up the mountain.

Evison had been hearing frequently about Mather and was happy to observe him at first hand. It was the beginning of a lifelong friendship. "Tall, erect, handsome, with white hair, he made a fine figure in the uniform of the National Park Service," Evison would recall many years later. "More important, he was a most 'meetable' person." Evison asserted his presence at the very first camping spot, near the snout of the Carbon Glacier, when he cooked prime steaks just by laying them on the coals of the campfire. Mather said he had never seen that done before — and the steaks were good.

On the last night of the trip, squatting beside a campfire on the shore of what is now named Mowich Lake, Mather offered a suggestion that would completely change Evison's life. He had come from several weeks in California, helping to promote the newly established Save-the-Redwoods League. "Why not get something going up here," asked Mather, "to save your own trees, especially along the highways?" A few days later he sketched out the framework of a save-the-trees organization. In due course this took shape as the Natural Park Association of Washington, with Evison as secretary and Mather as a member of the board and financial angel. In 1921 the association induced the legislature to establish the Washington state park system.

Evison later became the executive secretary of the National Conference of State Parks, another Mather brainchild, before joining the National Park Service as chief of information in Washington. After retiring in the mid-sixties, he became, for a decade or so, alumni editor of the *National Park Courier*, the bureau's house organ. He kept the Mather-Albright spirit alive and was thinking national parks, and believing in them, until he died in 1988 at the age of 96.

Early park rangers knew the outdoors, but not much about management of natural resources and people. As early as 1916, the year it was established, the National Park Service turned to the forestry school at a land-grant college, Colorado A&M, to staff its ranks with trained personnel. The faculty helped write the first park ranger examinations for the new agency and by the late 1920s the college became known as "the Ranger Factory."

A&M later became Colorado State University, but its emphasis remained on forestry — the production of a commodity —rather on preservation of nature for its own sake. Luckily, in 1934 John V.K. "Jack" Wagar joined the staff and founded programs in recreation and wildlife.

For thirty years Wagar instilled conservation principles and a land ethic in his students. He was a visionary considered strange by his colleagues yet inspiring to students. He wanted students to read newspapers regularly, to be able to speak and write, to get out of the classroom and test the world. "Outdoor recreation management," he wrote in 1966, two years after retiring, "is hampered by many who mistake recognition of happy participants (spending time and money) for understanding of areas and activities."

"I had always, for as far back as I can remember, been interested in origins," Gilbert Stucker recalled. "How did things begin? Here was this prairie, this street, those buldings — whatever I came in contact with — how did they start? How did things get going?"

Stucker was born in Chicago in 1914 and lived there until he was twenty-two. He spent many days reading in the public library, skipping school because it failed to encourage him in the search for origins. One day he discovered the book, *Principles of Paleontology*. Although he couldn't understand all its terminology, it told him about ancient forms of life, including some that had died out completely and others present in the modern world but in different form. It was the beginning, then and there, of his career in field paleontology. He didn't bother with college; he wanted to get directly to the subject matter, free of required courses and other distractions of structured education.

Over the years, Stucker conducted many field trips in the West, Southwest and Mexico for universities and major museums such as the Smithsonian Institution and American Museum of Natural History in New York. Ultimately, inevitably, his trail led to the most famous dinosaur repository in the world.

That "quarry" in northeastern Utah and western Colorado was discovered in 1909 by Earl Douglass, of the Carnegie Museum in Pittsburgh, during extensive explorations along the Green River. Douglass found eight bones half-embedded in weather-beaten rock, neatly attached together, unmistakeably part of the tail of a giant brontosaurus.

The finding by Douglass excited wonder about the ancient age when dinosaurs roamed. In 1915, eighty acres around the quarry were designated as Dinosaur National Monument; in 1923 it was closed to collecting to protect on site the skeletal remains embedded in the rocks. Then, in 1938, the monument was enlarged to more than 200,000 acres to preserve unimpaired the spectacular bordering high cliffs and canyons above the Green and Yampa rivers.

Stucker made his first visit to Dinosoaur in 1953, completely on his own, not primarily as a paleontologist but as a preservationist concerned with proposals to construct two dams across the rivers within the national monument. The dams were part of the construction program of the Bureau of Reclamation, an agency with strong political support in the West. Conservation leaders feared that allowing such a project in Dinosaur would place the entire national park system in jeopardy.

Deeply disturbed at the prospect of the dams, Stucker called on Horace Albright in his New York business office to broach an idea. Though long retired as director of the National Park Service, Albright remained involved and influential. Stucker told him that scientists were hopeful the government would develop the quarry and now was the time to do it.

"Why not use the quarry as a positive project, a platform from which to generate public interest and concern?" Stucker asked rhetorically. "Not only would we start working back into the cliff to look for dinosaur remains and expose them for future exhibit, but at the same time show people tremendous bones etched out in relief, bones of animals 140 million years old. We can see them right in the rock where they died before the rock solidified.

"We would tell the public, 'You may think this is wonderful, but it's only a very small part of the treasures in Dinosaur National Monument. Back in these canyons we have ocean beds with millions upon millions of remains of sea life — shells and corals, coral reefs, all sorts of remains of prehistoric life.

Although the quarry would not be touched by the flooding of these canyons, all the other formations of the earth's history — of which the quarry is just a very small sequence, a very small chapter — all that would be flooded out.' We would get people interested in the quarry and, through it, interested in the canyons and the threats to them."

Albright sent Stucker to talk with Conrad L. Wirth, then director of the National Park Service. Wirth listened and responded that he and his staff had been considering just such a project. And the year following, when it began, Stucker was offered, and accepted, a temporary appointment as ranger-naturalist. He would spend summers at the monument and winters at the American Museum of Natural History in New York as a specialist in paleontology. A four-man team, including Stucker, worked before public view on the north wall of the quarry, removing tons of rock with air-powered jack hammers and rotary rock drills, then roughing out bones with smaller chipping hammers and detailing them with hand tools. Visitors would ask questions, giving him the chance to lecture to large and small groups.

"I realized full well that when I discussed the proposed dams, I was exceeding my authority," Stucker recalled later. "I was supposed to explain the quarry to the visiting public, not ask people to write their congressmen. At one point park superintendent Jess Lombard called me into his office and said, 'I just had a telegram from the Secretary of the Interior directing that no park service employee is to discuss the threat of dams in Dinosaur National Monument. I know you've been talking against the dams. If you continue, I will have to separate you or discharge you. I have no choice.'

"But I knew that I must talk against the dams and somehow rode it through until the question was settled — and Dinosaur was saved."

Once it was over, Stucker was offered a permanent position with the National Park Service. He considered it carefully, but felt that sometime in future he might want to speak out and wouldn't be able to do so without risk. Instead, he went with the American Museum, conducting field studies in different parts of the continent. On his own time he continued his conservation work, joining efforts to add choice areas to the national park system: One of these, Fossil Butte, in Wyoming, preserving fish forty or fifty million years in laminated clays and silts, was declared a national monument in 1972. After retiring in 1979, Stucker became active in the National Parks and Conservation Association and served a term as chairman of its board.

The fossil quarry at Dinosaur National Monument is enclosed in a long museum of concrete and glass. In full public view, conservators work on the north wall, bringing fresh materials to light— tail vertebrae, rib and leg elements, foot bones, a complete hind leg, vertebrae columns. Visitors ask a variety of questions, including, "May I pet a bone?" An average of fifteen to twenty paleontologists come each year, from museums, universities, from all over the world.

"There's nothing like it in the world," said Tobe Wilkins, who in 1953 began working with Stucker on the rock wall and continued to do so for thirty-five years (and who Stucker credits for the greatest single contribution to the remarkable display of fossil remains). "It's like unwrapping a Christmas present; you never know what you're going to find. You uncover a piece of fossil — you're the first human to ever see it." No one knows the full value of paleontology. It is said to be a very careful, exact science, yet in years, or generations hence, specimens preserved may reveal much more than they do today, because of the sharpening of human intelligence. But the same holds for all the pre-history and history, of nature and human culture, in the national parks. Those values last and grow forever.

Looking Back, Looking Ahead

Reviewing the national parks from the days of discovery for me is like a trip "back to the future," with much to enjoy and maybe even more to learn.

National parks when they were new yielded discovery, adventure, and challenge. They should always do that. And they can, if we really want them to.

As the rest of the country becomes developed and supercivilized, national parks should be held apart, safeguarded to represent another side of America free of technology, commerce and crowds, a pioneer, self-reliant side of America.

"Without parks and outdoor life," as Enos Mills wrote, "all that is best in civilization will be smothered. To save ourselves — to enable us to live at our best and happiest — parks are necessary."

National parks are too much taken for granted, as though they've always been there, and therefore always will be with us. But it took vision to bring them into being, and it will take vision to assure their proper future.

I look back:

To 1864, when Congress responded to fears of destruction of prized natural wonders by granting to California for safekeeping Yosemite Valley and the Mariposa grove of giant sequoias.

To 1872, when the Yellowstone Act established the first national park, sparking a new kind of land ethic.

To 1916, when the National Parks Act created the National Park Service, and for the first time the federal government defined the specific intent of preserving unimpaired nature on a grand scale.

To the mid-1920s, when Congress voted to establish three national parks in the Southern Appalachians out of private lands (Great Smoky Mountains, Mammoth Cave, Shenandoah) — in contrast to parks in the West, from land already federally owned.

To the 1950s, when the proposed construction of dams in Dinosaur National Monument, though remote and little known, was defeated by a nationwide citizen campaign, protecting the integrity of all national parks.

To the post World War II expansion of the national park system to include lands formerly commercially exploited, most recently Redwood National Park, showing that nature and human healing hands can overcome past abuses.

These positive actions show what can be done. Rail travel has been reintroduced to the Grand Canyon, and should be to other parks as well. Rail travel makes for better access and better park experience than car travel.

John Muir lamented the day when Yosemite was opened to automobiles. That, he warned, would only bring crowds and city living with them, while Yosemite would be lost sight of, as if its thousand square miles of wonderful mountains, canyons, glaciers, forests, and songful falling rivers had no existence.

There should be fewer roads in the parks, and no off-road vehicles, no airplane or helicopter sightseeing disruptions of pioneering adventure.

The country needs more parks, all kinds of parks. Stephen T. Mather, first director of the National Park Service, was a booster of state parks. He wanted a state park located every hundred miles along the main highways leading to and supplementing national parks. Parks and open spaces should be located in and around towns and cities, providing the companionship of nature as part of life.

A national park is more than a place to play, but a refuge, sanctuary, a great outdoor cathedral of harmony and hope. It takes patience to get the best out of it, looking back into time, and ahead to the future with a desire to make it work.

Mount Ranier National Park
Tahoma Woods, Star Route
Ashford, Washington 98304

National Park Service
Pacific Northwest
Regional Office
601 4th and Pike Building
Seattle, Washington 98101
206/442-0170

MOUNT RAINIER
NATIONAL PARK

3.

3. Camped before a splendid backdrop, hungry tourists and their guide (stoically accepting a faceful of camp-fire smoke for the cameraman) pause at a fixed trail site.

4

4.   *A tenderfoot trail ride in Mt. Ranier foothills.*
5.   *Following spread: Hikers along two-rutted road absorb the grandeur.*

41

6

6. *Trail riders amidst a valley of wildflowers rimmed by snowcapped mountains.*

7. *Comet Falls.*

8. *Following spread: Mt. Rainier and Mowich Canyon.*

Mt. Rainier and Mowich [...]

8

9

9. *Sheer, vertical drop along the Glacier Trail.*

10

10. Sluiskan Falls.

Grand Canyon National Park
P.O. Box 129
Grand Canyon, Arizona 86203

National Park Service
Southwest
Regional Office
P.O. Box 728
Santa Fe, New Mexico 87501
505/988-6375

GRAND CANYON
NATIONAL PARK

The Grand Canyon Exploration: 1869

John Wesley Powell

The following account records the first attempt to traverse the awesome Grand Canyon. The 1869 achievement is even more notable in that the author, a member of the U.S. Geological survey, had lost his right arm in the Battle of Shiloh during the Civil War. This excerpt is taken directly from Powell's official 1875 account, **The Exploration of the Colorado River**.

August 13. We are now ready to start on our way down the Great Unknown. Our boats, tied to a common stake, are chafing each other, as they are tossed by the fretful river. They ride high and buoyant, for their loads are lighter than we could desire. We have but a month's rations remaining. The flour has been resifted through the mosquito-net sieve; the spoiled bacon has been dried, and the worst of it boiled; the few pounds of dried apples have been spread in the sun, and reshrunken to their normal bulk; the sugar has all melted, and gone on its way down the river; but we have a large sack of coffee. The lightening of the boats has this advantage; they will ride the waves better, and we shall have but little to carry when we make a portage.

We are three quarters of a mile in the depths of the earth, and the great river shrinks into insignificance, as it dashes its angry waves against the walls and cliffs, that rise to the world above; they are but puny ripples, and we but pigmies, running up and down the sands, or lost among the boulders. We have an unknown distance yet to run; an unknown river yet to explore. What falls there are, we know not; what rocks beset the channel we know not; what walls rise over the river, we know not. Ah, well! We may conjecture many things. The men talk as cheerfully as ever; jests are bandied about freely this morning; but to me the cheer is somber and the jests are ghastly.

With some eagerness, and some anxiety, and some misgiving, we enter the canyon below, and are carried along by the swift water through walls which rise from its very edge. They have the same structure as we noticed yesterday - tiers of irregular shelves below, and, above these, steep slopes to the foot of marble cliffs. We run six miles in a little more than half an hour, and emerge into a more open portion of the canyon, where high hills and ledges of rock intervene between the river and the distant walls. Just at the head of this open place the river runs across a dike; that is, a fissure in the rocks, open to depths below, has been filled with eruptive matter, and this, on cooling, was harder than the rocks through which the crevice was made, and, when these were washed away, the harder volcanic matter remained as a wall, and the river has cut a gateway through it several hundred feet high, and as many wide. As it crosses the wall, there is a fall below, and a bad rapid, filled with boulders of trap; so we stop to make a portage. Then we go, gliding by hills and ledges, with distant walls in view; sweeping past sharp angles of rock; stopping at a few points to examine rapids, which we find can be run, until we have made another five miles, when we land for dinner.

Then we let down with lines, over a long rapid, and start again. Once more the walls close in, and we find ourselves in a narrow gorge, the water again filling the channel, and very swift. With great care, and constant watchfulness, we proceed, making about four miles this afternoon, and camp in a cave.

August 14. At daybreak we walk down the bank of the river, on a little sandy beach, to take a view of a new feature in the canyon. Heretofore, hard rocks have given us bad river; soft rocks, smooth water; and a series of rocks harder than any we have experienced sets in. The river enters the granite!

We can see but a little way into the granite gorge, but it looks threatening.

After breakfast we enter on the waves. At the very introduction, it inspires awe. The canyon narrower than we have ever before seen it; the water is swifter; there are but few broken rocks in the channel; but the walls are set, on either side, with pinnacles and crags; and sharp, angular buttresses, bristling with wind and wave-polished spires, extend far out into the river.

Ledges of rocks jut into the stream, their tops sometimes just below the surface, sometimes rising few or many feet above; and island ledges, and island pinnacles, and island towers break the swift course of the

11

11. *Not surprisingly, early commercial
photographers were enamored of the
Grand Canyon and used models
extensively to dramatize heights or
illustrate the humbling qualities of its
splendor.*

stream into chutes, and eddies, and whirlpools. We soon reach a place where a creek comes in from the left, and just below, the channel is choked with boulders, which have washed down this lateral canyon and formed a dam, over which there is a fall of thirty or forty feet; but on the boulders we can get foothold, and we make a portage.

Three more such dams are found. Over one we make a portage; at the other two we find chutes, through which we can run.

As we proceed, the granite rises higher, until nearly a thousand feet of the lower part of the walls are composed of this rock.

About eleven o'clock we hear a great roar ahead, and approach it very cautiously. The sound grows louder and louder as we run, and at last we find ourselves above a long, broken fall, with ledges and pinnacles of rock obstructing the river. There is a descent of, perhaps, seventy-five or eighty feet in a third of a mile, and the rushing waters breaking into great waves on the rocks, and lash themselves into a mad, white foam. We can land just above, but there is no foothold on either side by which we can make a portage. It is nearly a thousand feet to the top of the granite, so it will be impossible to carry our boats around, though we can climb to the summit up a side gulch, and, passing along a mile or two, can descend to the river. This we find on examination; but such a portage would be impracticable for us, and we must run the rapid, or abandon the river. There is no hesitation. We step into our boats, push off and away we go, first on smooth but swift water, then we strike a glassy wave, and ride to its top, down again into the trough, up again on a higher wave, and down and up on waves higher and still higher, until we strike one just as it curls back, and a breaker rolls over our little boat. Still, on we speed, shooting past projecting rocks, till the little boat is caught in a whirlpool, and spun around several times. At last we pull out again into the stream, and now the other boats have passed us. The open compartment of the ''Emma Dean'' is filled with water, and every breaker rolls over us. Hurled back from a rock, now on this side, now on that, we are carried into an eddy, in which we struggle for a few minutes, and then out again, the breakers still rolling over us. Our boat is unmanageable, but she cannot sink, and we drift down another hundred yards, through breakers; how, we scarcely know. We find the other boats have turned into an eddy at the foot of the fall, and are waiting to catch us as we come, for the men have seen that our boat is swamped. They push out as we come near, and pull us in against the wall. We bail our boat, and on we go again.

The walls, now, are more than a mile in height - a vertical distance difficult to appreciate. Stand on the south steps of the Treasury building, in Washington, and look down Pennsylvania Avenue to the Capitol Park, and measure this distance overhead, and imagine cliffs to extend to that altitude, and you will understand what I mean; or, stand at Canal Street, in New York, and look up Broadway to Grace Church, and you have about the distance; or, stand at Lake Street bridge in Chicago, and look down to the Central Depot, and you have it again.

A thousand feet of this is up through granite crags, then steep slopes and perpendicular cliffs rise, one above another, to the summit. The gorge is black and narrow below, red and gray and flaring above, with crags and angular projections on the walls, which, cut in many places by side canyons, seem to be a vast wilderness of rocks. Down in these grand, gloomy depths we glide, ever listening, for the mad waters keep up their roar; ever watching, ever peering ahead, for the narrow canyon is winding, and the river is closed in so that we can see but a few hundred yards, and what there may be below we know not; but we listen for falls, and watch for rocks, or stop now and then, in the bay of a recess, to admire the gigantic scenery. And ever, as we go, there is some new pinnacle or tower, some crag or peak, some distant view of the upper plateau, some strange-shaped rock, or some deep, narrow side canyon. Then we come to another broken fall, which appears more difficult than the one we ran this morning.

A small creek comes in on the right, and the first fall of the water is over boulders, which have been carried down by this lateral stream. We land at its mouth, and stop for an hour or two to examine the fall. It seems possible to let down with lines, at least a part of the way, from point to point, along the right-hand wall. So we make a portage over the first rocks, and find footing on some boulders below. Then we let down one of the boats to the end of her line, when she reaches a corner of the projecting rock, to which one of the men clings, and steadies her, while I examine an eddy below. I think we can pass the other boats down by us, and catch them in the eddy. This is soon done and the men in the boats in the eddy pull us to their side. On the shore of this little eddy there is about two feet of gravel beach above the water. Standing on this beach, some of the men take the line of the little boat and let it drift down against another projecting angle. Here is a little shelf, on which a man from my boat climbs, and a shorter line is passed to him, and he fastens the boat to the side of the cliff. Then the second one is let down, bringing the line of the third. When the second boat is tied up, the two men standing on the beach above spring into the last boat, which is pulled up alongside of ours. Then we let down the boats, for twenty-five or thirty yards, by walking along the shelf, landing them again in the mouth of a side canyon. Just below this there is another pile of boulders, over which we make another portage. From the foot of these rocks we can climb to another shelf, forty or fifty feet above the water.

On this bench, we camp for the night. We find a few sticks, which have lodged in the rocks. It is raining hard, and we have no shelter, but kindle a fire and have our supper. We sit on the rocks all night, wrapped

12

12. *Venturing a little too near the Yawning Chasm, 1903. On Sentinel Point, 1906.*

Fathoming the depth of a vanished sea -
13. *Grand Canyon of Arizona from Hance's Cove, 1903.*

13

in our ponchos, getting what sleep we can.

August 15. This morning we find we can let down for three or four hundred yards, and it is managed in this way: We pass along the wall, by climbing from projecting point to point, sometimes near the water's edge, and other places, fifty or sixty feet above, and hold the boat with a line, while two men remain aboard, and prevent her from being dashed against the rocks, and keep the line from getting caught ont he wall. In two hours we have brought them all down, as far as it is possible, in this way. A few yards below, the river strikes with great violence against a projecting rock, and our boats are pulled up in a little bay above. We must now manage to pull out of this, and clear the point below. The little boat is held by the bow obliquely up the stream. We jump in, and pull out only a few strokes, and sweep clear of the dangerous rock. The other boats follow in the same manner, and the rapid is passed.

It is not easy to describe the labor of such navigation. We must prevent the waves from dashing the boats against the cliffs. Sometimes, where the river is swift, we must put a bight of rope about a rock, to pre-

vent her being snatched from us by a wave; but where the plunge is too great, or the chute too swift, we must let her leap, and catch her below, or the undertow will drag her under the falling water, and she sinks. Where we wish to run her out a little way from shore, through a channel between rocks, we first throw in little sticks of driftwood, and watch their course, to see where we must steer, so that she will pass the channel in safety. And so we hold, and let go, and pull, and lift, and ward, among rocks, around rocks, and over rocks.

And now we go on through this solemn, mysterious way. The river is very deep, the canyon very narrow, and still obstructed, so that there is no steady flow of the stream; but the waters wheel, and roll, and boil, and we are scarcely able to determine where we can go. Now, the boat is carried to the right, perhaps close to the wall; again, she is shot into the stream, and perhaps is dragged over to the other side, where, caught in a whirlpool, she spins about. We can neither land nor run as we please. The boats are entirely unmanageable; no order in their running can be preserved; now one, now another, is ahead, each crew laboring for its

55

own preservation. In such a place we come to another rapid. Two of the boats run it perforce. One succeeds in landing, but there is no foothold by which to make a portage, and she is pushed out again into the stream. The next minute a great reflex wave fills the open compartment; she is waterlogged, and drifts unmanageable. Breaker after breaker rolls over her, and one capsizes her. The men are thrown out; but they cling to the boat, and she drifts down some distance, alongside of us, and we are able to catch her. She is soon bailed out, and the men are aboard once more; but the oars are lost, so a pair from the ''Emma Dean'' is spared. Then for two miles we find smooth water.

Clouds are playing in the canyon today. Sometimes they roll down in great masses, filling the gorge with gloom; sometimes they hang above, from wall to wall, and cover the canyon with a roof of impending storm; and we can peer long distances up and down this canyon corridor, with its cloud roof overhead, its walls of black granite, and its river bright with the sheen of broken waters. Then, a gust of wind sweeps down a side gulch, and, making a rift in the clouds, reveals the blue heavens, and a stream of sunlight pours in. Then, the clouds drift away into the distance, and hang around crags, and peaks, and pinnacles, and towers, and walls, and cover them with a mantle, that lifts from time to time, and sets them all in sharp relief. Then, baby clouds creep out of side canyons, glide around points, and creep back again, into more distant gorges. Then, clouds, set in strata, across the canyon, with intervening vista views to cliffs and rocks beyond. The clouds are children of the heavens, and when they play among the rocks, they lift them to the region above.

It rains! Rapidly little rills are formed above, and these soon grow into brooks, and the brooks grow into creeks, and tumble over the walls in innumerable cascades, adding their wild music to the roar of the river. When the rain ceases, the rills, brooks, and creeks run dry. The waters that fall, during a rain, on these steep rocks, are gathered at once into the river; they could scarcely be poured in more suddenly, if some vast spout ran from the clouds to the stream itself. When a storm bursts over the canyon, a side gulch is dangerous, for a sudden flood may come, and the inpouring waters will raise the river, so as to hide the rocks before your eyes.

Early in the afternoon, we discover a stream, entering from the north, a clear, beautiful creek, coming down through a gorgeous red canyon. We land, and camp on a sand beach, above its mouth, under a great, overspreading tree, with willow-shaped leaves. . .

August 24. The canyon is wider today. The walls rise to a vertical height of nearly three thousand feet. In many places the river runs under a cliff, in great curves, forming amphitheaters, half dome-shaped.

Though the river is rapid, we meet with no serious obstructions, and run twenty miles. It is curious how anxious we are to make up our reckoning every time we stop, now that our diet is confined to plenty of coffee, very little spoiled flour, and very few driedap-

ples. It has come to be a race for a dinner. Still, we make such fine progress, all hands are in good cheer, but not a moment of daylight is lost.

August 25. We make twelve miles this morning, when we come to monuments of lava, standing in the river; low rocks, mostly, but some of them shafts more than a hundred feet high. Going on down, three or four miles, we find them increasing in number. Great quantities of cooled lava and many cinder cones are seen on either side; and then we come to an abrupt cataract. Just over the fall, on the right wall, a cinder cone, or extinct volcano, with a well-defined crater, stands on the very brink of the canyon. This doubtless, is the one we saw two or three days ago. From this volcano vast floods of lava have been poured down into the river and a stream of the molten rock has run up the canyon, three or four miles, and down, we know not how far. Just where it poured over the canyon wall is the fall. The whole north side, as far as we can see, is lined with the black basalt, and high up on the opposite wall are patches of the same material, resting on the benches, and filling old alcoves and caves, giving to the wall a spotted appearance.

The rocks are broken in two, along a line which here crosses the river, and the beds, which we have seen coming down the canyon for the last thirty miles, have dropped 800 feet, on the lower side of the line, forming what geologists call a fault. The volcanic cone stands directly over the fissure thus formed. On the side of the river opposite, mammoth springs burst out of this crevice, one or two hundred feet above the river, pouring in a stream quite equal in volume to the colorado Chiquito.

This stream seems to be loaded with carbonate of lime, and the water, evaporating, leaves an incrustation on the rocks; and this process has been continued for a long time, for extensive deposits are noticed, in which are basins, with bubbling springs. The water is salty.

We have to make a portage here, which is completed in about three hours, and on we go.

We have no difficulty as we float along, and I am able to observe the wonderful phenomena connected with this flood of lava. The canyon was doubtless filled to a height of twelve or fifteen hundred feet, perhaps by more than one flood. This would dam the water back; and in cutting through this great lava bed, a new channel has been formed, sometimes on one side, sometimes on the other. The cooled lava, being of firmer texture than the rocks of which the walls are composed, remains in some places; in others a narrow channel has been cut, leaving a line of basalt on either side. It is possible that the lava cooled faster on the sides against the walls, and that the centre ran out; but of this we can only conjecture. There are other places, where almost the whole of the lava is gone, patches of it only being seen where it has caught on the walls. As we float down, basalt has a fine, columnar structure, often in concentric prisms, and masses of these concentric columns have coalesced. In some places, when the flow occurred, the canyon was probably at about the same depth as it is now, for we can see where the basalt has rolled out on the sands, and, what seems curious to me, the sands are not melted or metamorphosed to any appreciable extent. In places the bed of the river is of sandstone or limestone, in other places of lava, showing that it has all been cut out again where the sandstones and limestones appear; but there is a little yet left where the bed is of lava.

What a conflict of water and fire there must have been here! Just imagine a river of molten rock, running down into a river of melted snow. What a seething and boiling of the waters; what clouds of steam rolled into the heavens!

Thirty-five miles today. Hurrah!

August 26. The canyon walls are steadily becoming higher as we advance. They are still bold, and nearly vertical up to the terrace. We still see evidence of the eruption discovered yesterday, but the thickness of the basalt is decreasing, as we go down the stream; yet it has been reinforced at points by streams that have come down from volcanoes standing on the terrace above, but which we cannot see from the river below. Since we left the Colorado Chiquito, we have seen no evidences that the tribe of Indians inhabiting the plateaus on either side ever come down to the river; but about eleven o'clock today we discover an Indian garden, at the foot of the wall on the right, just where a little stream, with a narrow flood plain, comes down through a side canyon. Along the valley, the Indians have planted corn, using the water which burst out in springs at the foot of the cliff, for irrigation. The corn is looking quite well, but is not sufficiently advanced to give us roasting ears; but there are some nice, green squashes. We carry ten or a dozen of these on board our boats, and hurriedly leave, not willing to be caught in the robbery, yet excusing ourselves by pleading our great want. We run down a short distance, to where we feel certain no Indians can follow; and what a kettle of squash sauce we make! True, we have no salt with which to season it, but it makes a fine addition to our unleavened bread and coffee. Never was fruit so sweet as these stolen squashes.

After dinner we push on again, making fine time, finding many rapids, but none so bad that we cannot run them with safety, and when we stop, just at dusk, and foot up our reckoning, we find we have run thirty-five miles again.

What a supper we make! unleavened bread, green squash sauce, and strong coffee. We have been for a few days on half rations, but we have no stint of roast squash.

A few days like this, and we are out of prison.

August 27. This morning the river takes a more southerly direction. The dip of the rocks is to the north, and we are rapidly running into lower formations. Unless our course changes, we shall very soon run again into the granite. This gives us some anxiety. Now and

14

14. *"Man Hath No Part In All This Glorious Work - From Grandview Hotel", circa 1905.*

then the river turns to the west, and excites hopes that are soon destroyed by another turn to the south. About nine o'clock we come to the dreaded rock. It is with no little misgiving that we see the river enter these black, hard walls. At its very entrance we have to make a portage; then we have to let down with lines past some ugly rocks. Then we run a mile or two farther, and then the rapids below can be seen.

About eleven o'clock we come to a place in the river where it seems much worse than any we have yet met in all its course. A little creek comes down from the left. We land first on the right, and clamber up over the granite pinnacles for a mile or two, but can see no way by which we can let down, and to run it would be sure destruction. After dinner we cross to examine it on the left. High above the river we can walk along on the top of the granite, which is broken off at the edge, and set with crags and pinnacles, so that it is very difficult to get a view of the river at all. In my eagerness to reach a point where I can see the roaring fall below, I go too far on the wall, and can neither advance nor retreat. I stand with one foot on a little projecting rock, and cling with my hand fixed in a little crevice. Finding I am caught here, suspended 400 feet above the river, into which I should fall if my footing fails, I call for help. The men come, and pass me a line, but I cannot let go of the rock long enough to take hold of it. Then they bring two or three of the largest oars. All this takes time which seems very precious to me; but at last they arrive. The blade of one of the oars is pushed into a little crevice in the rock beyond me, in such a manner that

15. *On Granger Point, 1906.*

they can hold me pressed against the wall. Then another is fixed in such a way that I can step on it, and thus I am extricated.

Still another hour is spent in examining the river from this side, but no good view of it is obtained, so now we return to the side that was first examined, and the afternoon is spent in clambering among the crags and pinnacles, and carefully scanning the river again. We find that the lateral streams have washed boulders into the river, so as to form a dam, over which the water makes a broken fall of eighteen or twenty feet; then there is a rapid beset with rocks, for two or three hundred yards, while, on the other side, points of the wall project into the river. Then there is a second fall below; how great, we cannot tell. Then there is a rapid, filled with huge rocks, for one or two hundred yards. At the bottom of it, from the right wall, a great rock projects quite halfway across the river. It has a sloping surface extending upstream, and the water, coming down with all the momentum gained in the falls and rapids above, rolls up this inclined plane many feet, and tumbles over to the left. I decide that it is possible to let down over the first fall, then run near the right cliff to a point just above the second, where we can pull out into a little chute, and, having run over that in safety, we must pull with all our power across the stream, to avoid the great rock below. On my return to the boat, I announce to the men that we are to run it in the morning. Then we cross the river, and go into camp for the night on some rocks, in the mouth of the little side canyon.

After supper Captain Howland asks to have a talk with me. We walk up the little creek a short distance, and I soon find that his object is to remonstrate against my determination to proceed. He thinks that we had better abandon the river here. Talking with him, I learn that his brother, William Dunn, and himself have determined to go no farther in the boats. So we return to camp. Nothing is said to the other men.

For the last two days, our course has not been plotted. I sit down and do this now for the purpose of finding where we are by dead reckoning. It is a clear night, and I take out the sextant to make observation for latitude, and find that the astronomic determination agrees very nearly with that of the plot — quite as closely as might be expected, from a meridian observation on a planet. In a direct line, we must be about forty-five miles from the mouth of the Rio Virgen. If we can reach that point, we know that there are settlements up that river about twenty miles. This forty-five miles, in a direct line, will probably be eighty or ninety in the meandering line of the river. But then we know that there is comparatively open country for many miles above the mouth of the Virgen, which is our point of destination.

As soon as I determine all this, I spread my plot on the sand, and wake Howland, who is sleeping down by the river, and show him where I suppose we are, and where several Mormon settlements are situated.

We have another short talk about the morrow, and he lies down again; but for me there is no sleep. All night long, I pace up and down a little path, on a few yards of sand beach, along by the river. Is it wise to go on? I go to the boats again, to look at our rations. I feel satisfied that we can get over the danger immediately before us; what there may be below I know not. From our outlook yesterday, on the cliffs, the canyon seemed to make another great bend to the south, and this, from our experience heretofore, means more and higher granite walls. I am not sure that we can climb out of the canyon here, and, when at the top of the wall, I know enough of the country to be certain that it is a desert of rock and sand, between this and the nearest Mormon town, which, on the most direct line, must be seventy-five miles away. True, the late rains have been favorable to us, should we go out, for the probabilities are that we shall find water still standing in holes, and, at one time, I almost conclude to leave the river. But for years I have been contemplating this trip. To leave the exploration unfinished, to say that there is a part of the canyon which I cannot explore, having already almost accomplished it, is more than I am willing to acknowledge, and I determine to go on.

I wake my brother, and tell him of Howland's determination, and he promises to stay with me; then I call up Hawkins, the cook, and he makes a like promise; then Sumner, and Bradley, and Hall, and they all agree to go on.

August 28. At last daylight comes, and we have breakfast, without a word being said about the future. The meal is solemn as a funeral. After breakfast, I ask the three men if they still think it best to leave us. The elder Howland thinks it is, and Dunn agrees with him. The younger Howland tries to persuade them to go on with the party, failing in which, he decides to go with his brother.

Then we cross the river. The small boat is very much disabled, and unseaworthy. With the loss of hands, consequent on the departure of the three men, we shall not be able to run all of the boats, so I decide to leave my "Emma Dean."

Two rifles and a shotgun are given to the men who are going out. I ask them to help themselves to the rations, and take what they think to be a fair share. This they refuse to do, saying they have no fear but that they can get something to eat; but Billy, the cook, has a pan of biscuits prepared for dinner, and these he leaves on a rock.

Before starting, we take our barometers, fossils, the minerals, and some ammunition from the boat, and leave them on the rocks. We are going over this place as light as possible. The three men help us lift our boats over a rock twenty-five or thirty feet high, and let them down again over the first fall, and now we are ready to start. The last thing before leaving, I write a letter to my wife, and give it to Howland. Sumner gives him his watch, directing that it be sent to his sister, should he not be heard from again. The records of the expedition have been kept in duplicate. One set of these is given to Howland, and now we are ready. For the last time, they entreat us not to go on, and tell us that it is madness to set out in this place; that we can never get safely through it; and, further, that the river turns again to the south into the granite, and a few miles of such rapids and falls will exhaust our entire stock of rations, and then it will be too late to climb out. Some tears are shed; it is rather a solemn parting; each party thinks the other is taking the dangerous course.

My old boat left, I go on board of the "Maid of the Canon." The three men climb a crag, that overhangs the river, to watch us off. The "Maid of the Canon" pushes out. We glide rapidly along the foot of the wall, just grazing one great rock, then pull out a little into the chute of the second fall, and plunge over it. The open compartment is filled when we strike the first wave below, but we cut through it, and then the men pull with all their power toward the left wall, and swing clear of the dangerous rock below all right. We are scarcely a minute in running it, and find that, although it looked bad from above, we have passed many places that were worse.

The other boat follows without more difficulty. We land at the first practicable point below, and fire our guns, as a signal to the men above that we have come over in safety. Here we remain a couple of hours, hoping that they will take the small boat and follow us. We are behind a curve in the canyon, and cannot see up to where we left them, and so we wait until their coming seems hopeless, and push on.

And now we have a succession of rapids and falls until noon, all of which we run in safety. Just after dinner we come to another bad place. A little stream comes in from the left, and below there is a fall, and still below another fall. Above, the river tumbles down, over and among the rocks, in whirlpools and great waves, and the waters are lashed into mad, white foam. We run along the left, above this, and soon see that we cannot get down on this side, but it seems possible to let down on the other. We pull upstream again, for two or three hundred yards, and cross. Now there is a bed of basalt on this northern side of the canyon, with a bold escarpment, that seems to be a hundred feet high. We can climb it, and walk along its summit to a point where we are just at the head of the fall. Here the basalt is broken down again, so it seems to us, and I direct the men to take a line to the top of the cliff, and let the boats down along the wall. One man remains in the boat, to keep her clear of the rocks, and prevent her line from being caught on the projecting angles. I climb the cliff, and pass along to a point just over the fall, and descend by broken rocks, and find that the break of the fall is above the break of the wall, so that we cannot land; and that still below the river is very bad, and that there is no possibility of a portage. Without waiting further to examine and determine what shall be done, I hasten back to the top of the cliff, to stop the boats from coming down. When I arrive, I find the men have let one of them down to the head of the fall. She is in swift water, and they are not able to pull her back; nor are they able to go on with the line, as it is not long enough to reach the higher part of the cliff, which is just before them; so they take a bight around a crag. I send two men back for the other line. The boat is in very swift water, and Bradley is standing in the open compartment, holding out his oar to prevent her from striking against the foot of the cliff. Now she shoots out into the stream, and up as far as the line will permit, and then, wheeling, drives headlong against the rock, then out and back again, now straining on the line, now striking against the rock. As soon as the second line is brought, we pass it down to him, but his attention is all taken up with his own situation, and he does not see that we are passing the line to him. I stand on a projecting rock, waving my hat to gain his attention, for my voice is drowned by the roaring of the falls. Just at this moment, I see him take his knife from its sheath, and step forward to cut the line. He has evidently decided that it is better to go over with the boat as it is, than to wait for her to be broken to pieces. As he leans over, the boat sheers again into the stream, the stem-post breaks away, and she is loose. With perfect composure Bradley seizes the great scull oar, places it in the stern rowlock, and pulls with all his power (and he is an athlete) to turn the bow of the boat downstream, for he wishes to go bow down, rather than to drift broadside on. One, two strokes he makes, and a third just as she goes over, and the boat is fairly turned, and she goes down almost beyond our sight, though we are more than a hundred feet above the river. Then she comes up again, on a great wave, and down and up, then around behind some great rocks, and is lost in the mad, white foam below. We stand frozen with fear, for we see no boat. Bradley is gone, so it seems. But now, away below, we see something coming out of the waves. It is evidently a boat. A moment more, and we see Bradley standing on deck, swinging his hat to show that he all right. But he is in a whirlpool. We have the stem-post of his boat attached to the line. How badly she may be disabled we know not. I direct Sumner and Powell to pass along the cliff, and see if they can reach him from below. Rhodes, Hall, and myself run to the other boat, jump aboard, and put out, and away we go over the falls. A wave rolls over us, and our boat is unmanageable. Another great wave strikes us, the boat rolls over, and tumbles and tosses, I know not how. All I know is that Bradley is picking us up. We soon have all right again, and row to the cliff, and wait until Sumner and Powell can come. After a difficult climb they reach us. We run two or three miles farther, and turn again to the northwest, continuing until night, when we have run out of granite once more.

August 29. We start very early this morning. The river still continues swift, but we have no serious difficulty and at twelve o'clock emerge from the Grand Canyon of the Colorado. We are in a valley now, and low mountains are seen in the distance, coming to the river below. We recognize this as the Grand Wash. A few years ago, a party of Mormons set out from St. George, Utah, taking with them a boat, and came down to the mouth of the Grand Wash, where they divided, a portion of the party crossing the river to explore the San Francisco Mountains. Three men - Hamblin, Miller, and Crosby - taking the boat, went on down the went on down the river to Callville, landing a few miles below the mouth of the Rio Virgen. We have their manuscript journal with us, and so the stream is comparatively well known.

Tonight we camp on the left bank, in a mesquite thicket.

The relief from danger, and the joy of success, are great. When he who has been chained by wounds to a hospital cot, until his canvas tent seems like a dungeon cell, until the groans of those who lie about, tortured with probe and knife, are piled up, a weight of horror on his ears that he cannot throw off, cannot forget, and until the stench of festering wounds and anesthetic drugs has filled the air with its loathsome burden, at last goes out into the open field, what a world he sees! How beautiful the sky; how bright the sunshine; what "floods of delirious music" pour from the throats of birds; how sweet the fragrance of earth, and tree, and blossom! The first hour of convalescent freedom seems rich recompense for all - pain, gloom, terror.

Something like this are the feelings we experience tonight. Ever before us has been an unknown danger, heavier than immediate peril. Every waking hour passed in the Grand Canyon has been one of toil. We have watched with deep solicitude the steady disappearance of our scant supply of rations, and from time to time have seen the river snatch a portion of the little left, while we were ahungered. And danger and toil were endured in those gloomy depths, where ofttimes the clouds hid the sky by day, and but a narrow zone of stars could be seen at night. Only during the few hours of deep sleep, consequent on hard labor, has the roar of the waters been hushed. Now the danger is over; now the toil has ceased; now the gloom has disappeared; now the firmament is bounded only by the horizon; and what a vast expanse of constellations can be seen!

The river rolls by us in silent majesty; the quiet of the camp is sweet; our joy is almost ecstasy. We sit till long after midnight, talking of the Grand Canyon, talking of home.

16.   Apache Indian posed above the Colorado River.

16

17

17. *"The 'Rendezvous' Hotel El Tovar, where tourists meet informally,"* circa 1905.

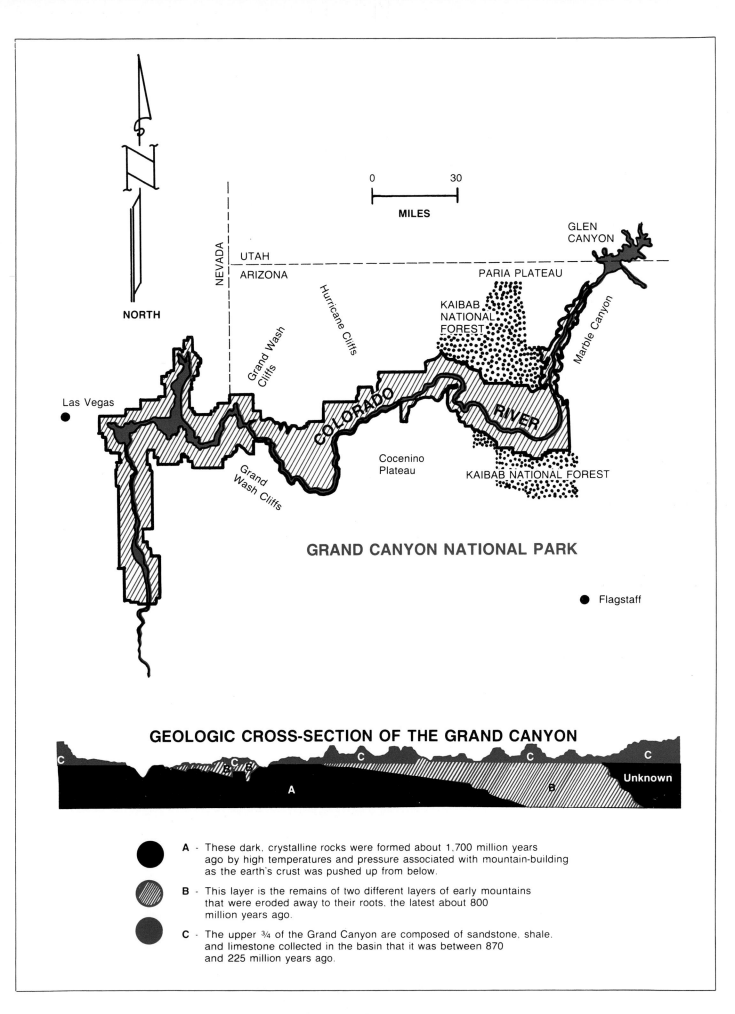

NORTH

NEVADA

UTAH

ARIZONA

Hurricane Cliffs

Grand Wash Cliffs

0   30

MILES

GLEN CANYON

PARIA PLATEAU

KAIBAB NATIONAL FOREST

Marble Canyon

Las Vegas

COLORADO

RIVER

Grand Wash Cliffs

Cocenino Plateau

KAIBAB NATIONAL FOREST

GRAND CANYON NATIONAL PARK

● Flagstaff

GEOLOGIC CROSS-SECTION OF THE GRAND CANYON

C   C B B   C   C   C

A

B

Unknown

A - These dark, crystalline rocks were formed about 1,700 million years ago by high temperatures and pressure associated with mountain-building as the earth's crust was pushed up from below.

B - This layer is the remains of two different layers of early mountains that were eroded away to their roots, the latest about 800 million years ago.

C - The upper ¾ of the Grand Canyon are composed of sandstone, shale, and limestone collected in the basin that it was between 870 and 225 million years ago.

Glacier National Park
West Glacier, Montana 59936

National Park Service
Pacific Northwest
Regional Office
601 4th and Pike Building
Seattle, Washington 98101
206/442-0170

GLACIER NATIONAL PARK

18

19

18. *"The Great Vertical Wall of the north
    face of Goathaunt Mountain."*

19. *Harrison Glacier*

20. *Following spread: A view of the cliffs from Lake Avalanche.*

Yellowstone National Park
P.O. Box 168
Yellowstone National Park,
Wyoming 82190

National Park Service
Southwest
Regional Office
P.O. Box 728
Santa Fe, New Mexico 87501
505/988-6375

YELLOWSTONE
NATIONAL PARK

21

22

21. *Amidst the amazing Yellowstone geysers, circa 1900.*

22. *"Gateway-Entrance to Yellowstone National Park", 1904.*

LOST IN THE
YELLOWSTONE: 1870

Truman C. Everts

During the late summer of 1870, the Doane-Washburn expedition set out to explore the strange and awesome Yellowstone territory. The group, comprised of U.S. Cavalry and otherwise hardy members, included one Truman C. Everts. Unlike his traveling companions, Everts was uniquely unfit for such an expedition. Fifty-four years of age, badly nearsighted and physically unfit for mountain travel, he lost contact with the rest of the party within a maze of blowdowns only several days into the forbidding country. For the next 37 days he would roam the mountains, meadows, lakes, rivers and geysers of the vast Yellowstone. Although near death, he still could not ignore the grandeur of the country around him. Following his rescue, he wrote the following journal of events of his harrowing experience in the wilderness. Everts died peacefully in 1901 at the age of 85.

Doane: ***First day-August 22, 1870*** We left Fort Ellis taking the road to the Yellowstone River, in an easterly direction. This road follows the general course of the East Gallatin, over a hilly country of limestone formation, with pine timber on the northern slopes. The ravines and small valleys are grown up with quaking aspens and willows.

Second day-August 23 Crossing a low ridge, we came in full sight of the Yellowstone Valley and stream, an extremely grand vista of some thirty miles shut in by volcanic mountains of immense height.

Third day-August 24 Several of the party were very successful during the morning in fishing for trout, of which we afterward had an abundant and continued supply.

Fifth day-August 26 We left camp at 11 o'clock a.m., and crossed Gardiner's River. Finding the canon impassable passed over serveral high spurs, over which the way was much obstructed by falling timber, and reached, at an elevation of 7,331 feet, an immense rolling plateau. The river breaks through in a winding and impassable canon of trachyte lava over 2,000 feet iin depth. Standing on the brink of the chasm the heavy roaring of the imprisoned river comes to the ear only in a sort of hollow, hungry growl. Everything beneath has a weird and deceptive appearance. The water does not look like water, but like oil. Bald eagles have their eyries, from which we can see them swooping still further into the depths to rob the ospreys of their hard-earned trout. It is grand, gloomy and terrible; a solitude peopled with fantastic ideas; an empire of shadows and of turmoil.

Twelfth day-September 2 On the slope of a small and steep wooded ravine is the crater of a mud volcano, 30 feet in diameter at the rim....Heavy volumes of steam escape from this opening, ascending to a height of 300 feet. From far down in the earth came a jarring sound, in regular beats of five seconds, with a concussion that shook the ground at two hundred yards....

Eighteenth day-September 8 ...The standing forest is very dense; the pack animals ran between trees, often wedging themselves in so tightly as to require some trouble in extricating them; serveral of the packs burst...Our faces were scratched, clothes torn, and limbs bruised squeezing through between saplings...Messrs. Hedges and Stickney wandered off from the party in the morning, but struck the shore of the lake and followed it, meeting us shortly after going into camp. In the evening a grizzly bear, with cubs, was roused by some of the party, but as they had not lost any bears, she got away with her interesting family undisturbed.

Nineteenth day-September 9 We moved in a westerly course over the summit of a high promontory, thence descending into a narrow open valley, and crossing a small stream rising in the promontory between two arms of the lake five miles in diameter. This stream is about 70 feet wide, 3 feet in depth, and is the main fork of Snake River.

On going into camp it was discovered that a pack-horse was missing. This animal, a small Cayuse, had been uniformly unfortunate, miring down in marshes, tumbling over log-heaps, and rolling endwise down steep banks; he was found a couple of miles back firmly wedged between two trees. Mr. Everts did not come

23

24

23, 24, & 25 Picnicking tourists, tack and Yellowstone teamsters, circa 1903.

25

in with the rest of the party, and men sent back on the trail found no traces of him. We fired signal guns, and kept watch fires during the night but without success. Supposing that he had passed to the right or left, we moved on the next day, leaving men behind on the trail.

EVERTS: *September 9* On the day that I found myself separated from the company, and for several days previous, our course had been impeded by the dense growth of the pine forest, and occasional large tracts of fallen timber, frequently rendering our progress almost impossible. Whenever we came to one of these immense windfalls, each man engaged in the pursuit of a passage through it, and it was while thus employed, and with the idea that I had found one, that I strayed out of sight and hearing of my comrades. We had a toilsome day. It was quite late in the afternoon. As separations like this had frequently occurred, it gave me no alarm, and I rode on, fully confident of soon rejoining the company, or of finding their camp. I came up with the pack-horse, which Mr. Langford afterwards recovered, and tried to drive him along, but failing to do so, and my eyesight being defective, I spurred forward. This incident tended to accelerate my speed. I rode on...until darkness overtook me in the dense forest. I had no doubt of being with the party at breakfast the next morning. I selected a spot for a comfortable repose, picketed my horse, built a fire, and went to sleep.

The next morning I rose at early dawn, saddled and mounted my horse, and took my course in the supposed direction of the camp. Our ride of the previous day had been up a peninsula jutting into the lake, for the shore of which I started, with the expectation of finding my friends camped on the beach. The forest was quite dark, and the trees so thick, that it was only by a slow process I could get through them at all. In searching for the trail I became somewhat confused. The falling foliage of the pine had obliterated every trace of travel. I was obliged frequently to dismount, and examine the ground for the faintest indications. Coming to an opening, from which I could see several vistas, I dismounted for the purpose of selecting one leading in the direction that I had chosen, and leaving my horse unhitched, as had always been my custom, walked a few rods into the forest. While surveying the ground my horse took fright, and I turned around in time to see him disappearing at full speed among the trees. That was the last I ever saw of him. It was yet quite dark. My blankets, gun, pistols, fishing tackle, matches- everything except the clothing on my person, a couple of knives, and a small opera-glass were attached to the saddle.

Instead of following up the pursuit of their camp, I engaged in an effort to recover my horse. Half a day's search convinced me of its impracticability. I wrote and posted in an open space several notices, which, if my friends should chance to see, would inform them of my condition and the route I had taken, and then struck out into the forest in the supposed direction of their camp. As the day wore on without any discovery, alarm took the place of anxiety at the prospect of another night alone in the wilderness, and this time without food or fire. But even this dismal foreboding was cheered by the hope that I should soon rejoin my companions, who would laugh at my adventure, and incorporate it as a thrilling episode into the journal of our trip. When I began to realize that my condition was one of actual peril, I banished from my mind all fear of an unfavorable result. Seating myself on a log, I recalled every foot of the way I had traveled since the separation from my friends, and the most probable opinion I could form of their whereabouts was, that they had, by a course but little different from mine, passed by the spot where I had posted the notices, learned of my disaster, and were waiting for me to rejoin them there, or searching for me in that vicinity. A night must be spent amid the prostrate trunks before my return could be accomplished. At no time during my period of exile did I experience so much mental suffering from the cravings of hunger as when, exhausted with this long day of fruitless search, I resigned myself to a couch of pine foliage in the pitchy darkness of a thicket of small trees. The wind sighed mournfully through the pines. The forest seemed alive with the screeching of night birds, the angry barking of coyotes, and the prolonged, dismal howl of the gray wolf.

DOANE: *Twentieth day-September 10* We broke camp at 10 a.m., taking a westerly course through fallen timber and over steep ridges, striking a long, slender arm of the lake in the afternoon; camped on this inlet — distance, 5 miles. Parties then went back on the trail, and laterally, hunting Mr. Everts. Messrs. Hauser and Langford ascended a high peak near camp and fired the woods, in hope of giving him a point of direction. We also fired signal guns during the night. In the evening large numbers of fish were caught, Private Williamson catching fifty-two large trout, all that two men could carry, in less than an hour. The night passed away and the missing man did not come. In the early morning we were serenaded by a couple of lions, their melancholy voices echoing through the heavy forest with a peculiar, wild, and mournful sound. We had blazed trees at all our camps throughout the whole trip, leaving on each a record, with date, route, and distances marked on the hewn sections. Here we also hung up in sight a few rations, hoping Mr. Everts might strike our trail and follow after we had gone.

EVERTS: *September 11* Early the next morning I rose unrefreshed, and pursued my weary way over the prostrate trunks. It was noon when I reached the spot where my notices were posted. No one had been there. My disappointment was almost overwhelming. For the first time, I realized that I was lost. Then came a crushing sense of destitution. No food, no fire; no means to procure either; alone in an unexplored wilderness, one hundred and fifty miles from the nearest human abode, surrounded by wild beasts, and famishing with hunger.

The hope of finding the party still controlled my plans. I thought, by traversing the peninsula centrally, at intervals throughout the next day.

EVERTS: *September 12*   I was roused by a marked change in the atmosphere. One of those dreary storms of mingled snow and rain, common to these high latitudes, set in. My clothing, which had been much torn, exposed my person to its 'pitiless peltings.' An easterly wind, rising to a gale, admonished me that it would be furious and of long duration. I could find no better shelter than the spreading branches of a spruce tree, under which, covered with earth and boughs, I lay during the two succeeding days; the storm, meanwhile, raging with unabated violence. While thus exposed, and suffering from cold and hunger, a little benumbed bird, not larger than a snow-bird, hopped within my reach. I instantly seized and killed it, and, plucking its feathers, ate it raw. It was a delicious meal for a half-starved man.

DOANE: *Twenty-second day—September 12*   Today parties went out in couples on the search. Messrs. Smith and Trumbull followed the lake shore around the head of the promontory to within sight of our previous camp. They returned in the evening and reported having seen human footsteps in the sands of the beach.

Twenty-third day—September 13   The snowy weather continued with intervals of hail and rain; large fires were kept up, and the search continued…. Messrs. Hauser and Gillette returned in the evening, unsuccessful in their search. The snow, hail, and rain, by turns, continued, and lions were again heard during the night.

Twenty-fourth day—September 14   We remained close in camp; the weather continued stormy; the snow was now twenty inches deep, and fell almost constantly; our pavilion tent served us admirably; without it we should have suffered great inconveniences for lack of shelter. The water-fowl of the lake deserve a passing notice. These include swans, pelicans, gulls, Canada geese, brants, and many varieties of ducks and dippers. There are also herons and sand-hill cranes. Of pelicans, immense numbers sail in fleets along the lake, incompany with the majestic swan. The common birds of the basin are eagles, hawks, ravens, ospreys, prairie chickens, and grouse. Of animals, I saw several species of squirrels and weasels which do not appear in the books.

EVERTS: *September 15*   Taking advantage of a lull in the elements, on the morning of the third day I rose early and started in the direction of a large group of hot springs which were steaming under the shadow of Mount Everts. The distance I traveled could not have been less than ten miles. Long before I reached the wonderful cluster of natural caldrons, the storm had recommenced. Chilled through, with my clothing thoroughly saturated, I lay down under a tree upon the heated incrustation until completely warmed. My heels and the sides of my feet were frozen. As soon as warmth had permeated my system, and I had quieted my appetite with a few thistle-roots, I took a survey of my surroundings, and selected a spot between two springs sufficiently asunder to afford heat at my head and feet. On this spot I built a bower of pine branches, spread its incrusted surface with fallen foliage and small boughs, and stowed myself away to await the close of the storm. Thistles were abundant, and I had fed upon them long enough to realize that they would, for a while at least, sustain life. In convenient proximity to my abode was a small, round, boiling spring, which I called my dinner pot, and in which, from time to time, I cooked my roots. This establishment, the best I could improvise with the means at hand, I occupied seven days-the first three of which were darkened by one of the most furious storms I ever saw. The vapor which supplied me with warmth saturated my clothing with its condensations. I was enveloped in a perpetual steam bath. At first this was barely preferable to the storm, but I soon became accustomed to it, and before I left, though thoroughly parboiled, actually enjoyed it.

DOANE: *Twenty-fifth day—September 15*   The snow storm abated, clouds hung overhead in heavy masses, an oppressive dampness pervaded the atmosphere, the snow melted away rapidly under the influence of a warm wind from the west.

Twenty-sixth day—September 16   We moved around the arm of the lake to the hot springs previously described, camping near them; distance; 5 miles.

Twenty-seventh day—September 17   Before leaving camp a council was held, which resulted in our leaving Mr. Gillette, with Privates Moore and Williamson, to make a final effort in the search of Mr. Everts. They were provided with one pack mule and ten days rations. They were to go back to Bozeman by our former route, or at discretion make a search and follow on our trail.

EVERTS: *September 16—23*   Nothing gave me more concern than the want of fire. An escape without it was simply impossible. It was indispensable as a protection against night attacks form wild beasts. Exposure to another storm like the one just over would destroy my life as this one would have done, but for the warmth derived from the springs. As I lay in my bower anxiously waiting the disappearance of the snow, which had fallen to the depth of a foot or more, a gleam of sunshine lit up the bosom of the lake, and with it the thought flashed upon my mind that I could, with a lens from my opera glasses, get fire from Heaven. Oh, happy, life renewing thought! Instantly subjecting it to the test of experiment, when I saw the smoke curl from the bit of dry wood in my fingers, I felt, if the whole world were offered me for it, I would cast it all aside before parting with that little spark. I was now the happy possessor of food and fire. These would carry me through.

My stay at the springs was prolonged several days by an accident that befell me on the third night after my arrival there. An unlucky movement while asleep broke the crust on which I reposed, and the hot steam, pouring upon my hip, scalded it severely before I could escape. This new affliction, added to my frost-bitten feet, already festering, was the cause of frequent delay and unceasing pain through all my wanderings. After obtaining fire, I set to work making preparations for

26

26. *Some of the famous Yellowstone bears;
eight blacks roam for handouts near the
Lake Hotel. Note tourist in extreme right
foreground.*

I would be enabled to strike the shore of the lake in advance of their camp, and near the point of departure for the Madison (River). Acting upon this impression, I rose from a sleepless couch, and pursued my way through the timber-entangled forest. A feeling of weakness took the place of hunger...

It was mid-day when I emerged from the forest into an open space at the foot of the peninsula. A broad lake of beautiful curvature, with magnificent surroundings, lay before me, glittering in the sunbeams. It was full twelve miles in circumference. A wide belt of sand formed the margin which I was approaching, directly opposite to which, rising seemingly from the very depths of the water, towered the loftiest peak of a range of mountains apparently interminable. The ascending vapor from innumerable hot springs, and the sparkling jet of a single geyser, added the feature of novelty to one of the grandest landscapes I ever beheld. Nor was the life of the scene less noticeable than its other attractions. Large flocks of swans and other water-fowl were sporting on the quiet surface of the lake; otters in great numbers performed the most amusing aquatic evolutions; mink and beaver swam around unscared, in most grotesque confusion. Deer, elk, and mountain sheep stared at me, manifesting more surprise than fear at my presence among them. Seen under favorable circumstances, this assemblage of grandeur, beauty, and novelty would have been transporting; but jaded with travel, famishing with hunger, and distressed with anxiety, I was in no humor for ecstasy...

The lake was at least one thousand feet lower than the highest point of the peninsula, and several hundred feet below the level of Yellowstone Lake. I recognized the mountain which overshadowed it as the landmark which, a few days before, had received from Gen. Washburn the name of Mount Everts; it is associated with some of the most agreeable and terrible incidents of my exile...

During the first two days, the fear of meeting with Indians gave me considerable anxiety; but when conscious of being lost, there was nothing I so much desired as to fall in with a lodge of Bannacks (Bannocks) or Crows. Having nothing to tempt their cupidity, they would do me no harm, and, with the promise of reward, would probably minister to my wants and aid my deliverance. Imagine my delight, while gazing upon the animated expanse of water, at seeing sail out from a distant point a large canoe containing a single oarsman. It was rapidly approaching the shore where I was seated. With hurried steps I paced the beach to meet it, all my energies stimulated by the assurance it gave of food, safety, and restoration to friends. As I drew near to it it turned towards the shore, and oh! bitter dissapointment, the object which my eager fancy had transformed into an angel of relief stalked from the water, an enormous pelican, flapped its dragon-wings as if in mockery of my sorrow, and flew to a solitary point farther up the lake. This little incident quite unmanned me. But night was fast approaching, and darkness would come

with it. While looking for a spot where I might repose in safety, my attention was attracted to a small green plant of so lively a hue as to form a striking contrast with the deep pine foliage. For closer examination I pulled it up by the root, which was long and tapering, not unlike a radish. It was a thistle. I tasted it; it was palatable and nutritious. My appetite craved it, and the first meal in four days was made on thistle roots. Overjoyed at this discovery, with hunger allayed, I stretched myself under a tree, upon the foliage which had partially filled a space between contiguous trunks, and fell asleep. How long I slept I know not; but suddenly I was roused by a loud, shrill scream, like that of a human being in distress, poured, seemingly, into the very portals of my ear. There was no mistaking that fearful voice. I had been deceived by and answered it a dozen times while threading the forest, with the belief that it was a friendly signal. It was the screech of a mountain lion, so alarmingly near as to cause every nerve to thrill with terror. To yell in return, seize with convulsive grasp the limbs of the friendly tree, and swing myself into it, was the work of the moment. Scrambling hurriedly from limb to limb, I was soon as near the top as safety would permit. The savage beast was snuffing and growling below, apparently on the very spot I had just abandoned. I answered every growl with a responsive scream. Terrified at the delay and pawing of the beast, I increased my voice to its utmost volume, broke branches from the limbs, and, in the impotency of fright, madly hurled them at the spot whence the continued howlings proceeded.

All in vain. The terrible creature pursued his walk around the tree, lashing the ground with his tail, and prolonging his howlings almost to a roar. It was too dark to see, but the movements of the lion kept me apprised of its position. Whenever I heard it on one side of the tree I speedily changed to the opposite. Moments passed with me like hours. After a lapse of time which I cannot estimate, the beast gave a spring into the thicket and screaming into the forest. My deliverance was effected.

Had strength permitted, I should have retained my perch till daylight, but with the consciousness of escape from the jaws of the ferocious brute came a sense of overpowering weakness which almost palsied me, and made my descent from the tree both difficult and dangerous. Incredible as it may seem, I lay down in my old bed, and was soon lost in a slumber so profound that I did not awake until after daylight.

DOANE: *Twenty-first day-September 11* After an easy ride in a direct line of seven miles, we reached the extreme westerly and longest arm of the lake (West Thumb), a lovely bay of water, six miles across, and with steam jets rising at its southern extremity in great numbers...We camped on the arm of the great lake three miles north of its extremity, and on the east side. Here we remained in camp during the 12th, 13th, 14th, and 15th, searching constantly for Mr. Everts. During the night a heavy snow-storm set in, which continued

27. *"Last remnants of the American Bison"* 1903.

28. *Following spread: Yellowstone River, circa 1905.*

28

as early departure as my condition would permit. I had lost both knives since parting from the company, but I now made a convenient substitute by sharpening the tongue of a buckle which I cut from my vest. With this I cut the legs and counters from my boots, making of them a passable pair of slippers, which I fastened to my feet as firmly as I could with strips of bark. With the ravelings of a lined handkerchief, aided by the magic buckle-tongue, I mended my clothing. Of the same material I made a fish-line. I made of a pin that I found in my coat a fish-hook, and, by sewing up the bottoms of my boot legs, constructed a very good pair of pouches to carry my food in, fastening them to my belt by the straps.

Thus accoutered, on the morning of the eighth day after my arrival at the springs I bade them a final farewell, and started on my course directly across that portion of the neck of the peninsula between me and the southeast arm of Yellowstone Lake. It was a beautiful morning. The sun shone bright and warm, and there was a freshness in the atmosphere truly exhilarating.

A change in the wind and an overcast sky, accompanied by cold, brought with them a need of warmth. I drew out my lens and touchwood, but alas! there was no sun. I sat down on a log to await his friendly appearance. Hours passed; he did not come. Night, cold, freezing night, set in, and found me exposed to all its terrors. A bleak hillside sparsely covered with pines afforded poor accommodations for a half-clad, famishing man. I could only keep from freezing by the most active exertion in walking, rubbing, and striking my benumbed feet and hands against the logs. It seemed the longest, most terrible night of my life, and glad was I when the approaching dawn enabled me to commence retracing my steps to Bessie Lake. I arrived there at noon, built my first fire on the beach, and remained by it, recuperating, for the succeeding two days.

The faint hope that my friends might be delayed by their search for me until I could rejoin them now forsook me altogether. I made my arrangements independent of it. Either of three directions I might take would effect my escape, if life and strength held out. I drew upon the sand of the beach a map of these several courses with reference to my starting-point from the lake, and considered well the difficulties each would present. One was to follow Snake River a distance of one hundred miles or more to Eagle Rock bridge; another, to cross the country between the southern shore of Yellowstone Lake and the Madison Mountains, by scaling which I could easily reach the settlements in the Madison Valley; and the other, to retrace my journey over the long and discouraging route by which I had entered the country. Of these routes the last-mentioned seemed the least inviting, probably because I had so recently traversed it, and was familiar with its difficulties. I had heard and read so much concerning the desolation and elemental upheavals and violent waters of the upper valley of the Snake, that I dared not attempt to return in that direction. The route by

the Madison Range, encumbered by the single obstruction of the mountain barrier, was much the shortest, and so, most unwisely as will hereafter appear, I adopted it.

Filling my pouches with thistle-roots, I took a parting survey of the little solitude that had afforded me food and fire the preceding ten days, and with something of that melancholy feeling experienced by one who leaves his home to grapple with untried adventures, started for the nearest point on Yellowstone Lake. All that day I traveled over timber-heaps, amid tree-tops, and through thickets. At noon I took the precaution to obtain fire. With a brand which I kept alive by frequent blowing, and constant waving to and fro, at a late hour in the afternoon, faint and exhausted, I kindled a fire for the night on the only vacant spot I could find amid a dense wilderness of pines. The deep gloom of the forest, in the spectral light which revealed on all sides of me a compact and unending growth of trunks, and an impervious canopy of somber foliage; the shrieking of night-birds; the supernaturally human scream of the mountain lion; the prolonged howl of the wolf, made me insensible to all other forms of suffering.

The burn on my hip was so inflamed that I could only sleep in a sitting posture. Seated with my back against a tree, the smoke from the fire almost enveloping me in its suffocating folds, I vainly tried, amid the din and uproar of this horrible serenade, to woo the drowsy god. My imagination was instinct with terror. At one moment it seemed as if, in the density of a thicket, I could see the blazing eyes of a formidable forest monster fixed upon me, preparatory to a deadly leap; at another I fancied that I heard the swift approach of a pack of yelping wolves through the distant brushwood, which in a few moments would tear me limb from limb. Whenever, by fatigue and weakness, my terrors yielded to drowsiness, the least noise roused me to a sense of the hideousness of my condition. Once, in a fitful slumber, I fell forward into the fire, and inflicted a wretched burn on my hand.

Another day of unceasing toil among the tree-tops and thickets overtook me, near sunset, standing upon a lofty headland jutting into the lake, and commanding a magnificent prospect of the mountains and valley over an immense area. In front of me, at a distance of fifty miles away, in the clear blue of the horizon, rose the arrowy peaks of the three Tetons. On the right, and apparently in close proximity to the eminence I occupied, rolled the picturesque range of the Madison scarred with clefts, ravines, gorges, and canyons, each of which glittered in the sunlight or deepened in shadow as the fitful rays of the descending luminary glanced along their varied rocky irregularities. Above where I stood were the lofty domes of Mounts Langord and Doane, marking the limits of that wonderful barrier which had so long defied human power in its efforts to subdue it. Rising seemingly from the promontory which favored my vision was the familiar summit of Mount Everts, at the base of which I had dwelt so long,

29. *Early tourists were allowed within close proximity of most geysers. Simple wooden stairs and deck separate viewers from active geyser.*

closure of mountains and lake, scarred and seamed with the grotesque ridges, rocky escarpments, undulating hillocks, miniature lakes, and steaming with hot springs, produced by the volcanic forces of a former era, lay spreadout before me like a vast panorama. I doubt if distress and suffering can ever entirely obliterate all sense of natural grandeur and magnificence. Lost in the wonder and admiration inspired by this vast world of beauties, I nearly forgot to improve the few moments of remaining sunshine to obtain fire. With a lighted brand in my hand, I effected a most difficult and arduous descent of the abrupt and stony headland to the beach of the lake. The sand was soft and yielding. I kindled a fire, and removing the stiffened slippers from my feet, attached them to my belt, and wandered barefoot along the sandy shore to gather wood for the night. The dry, warm sand was most grateful to my lacerated and festering feet, and for a long time after my wood-pile was supplied, I sat with them uncovered. At length, conscious of the need of every possible protection from the freezing night atmosphere, I sought my

belt for the slippers, and one was missing. In gathering the wood it had become detached, and was lost. Darkness was closing over the landscape, when, sorely disheartened with the thought of passing the night with one foot exposed to a freezing temperature, I commenced a search for the missing slipper. I knew I could not travel a day without it. Fearful that it had been dropped into the lake, and been carried by some recurrent wave beyond recovery, my search for an hour among fallen trees and bushes, up the hillside and along the beach, in darkness and with flaming brands, at one moment crawling on hands and feet into a brush-heap, another peering among logs and bushes and stones, was filled with anxiety and dismay. Success at length rewarded my perseverance, and no language can describe the joy with which I drew the cause of so much distress from beneath the limb that, as I passed, had torn it from my belt. With a feeling of great relief, I now sat down in the sand, my back to a log, and listened to the dash and roar of the waves. It was a wild lullaby, but had no terrors for a worn-out man. I never passed a night of more refreshing sleep. When I awoke my fire was extinguished save a few embers, which I soon fanned into a cheerful flame. I ate breakfast with some relish, and started along the beach in pursuit of a camp.

Buoyed by the hope of finding food and counsel, and another night of undisturbed slumber in the sand, I resumed my journey along the shore, and at noon found the camp last occupied by my friends on the lake. I struck their trail in the sand some time before I came to it. A thorough search for food in the trees revealed nothing, and no notice to apprise me of their movements could be seen. A dinner-fork, which afterwards proved to be of infinite service in digging roots, and a yeast-powder can, which would hold half a pint, and which I converted into a drinking cup and dinner pot, were the only evidences that the spot had ever been visited by civilized man. "Oh!" thought I, "why did they forget to leave me food!" it never occurring to me that they might have cached it. I left the camp in deep dejection, (and followed) my steps along the beach. An hour of sunshine in the afternoon enabled me to procure fire, which, in the usual manner, I carried to my camping place. There I built a fire, and to protect myself from the wind, which was blowing violently, lashing the lake into foam, I made a bower of pine boughs, crept under it, and very soon fell asleep. How long I slept I know not, but I was aroused by the snapping and cracking of the burning foliage, to find my shelter and the adjacent forest in a broad sheet of flame. My left hand was badly burned, and my hair singed closer than a barber would have trimmed it, while making my escape from the semicircle of burning trees. Among the disasters of this fire, there was none I felt more seriously than the loss of my buckle-tongue knife, my pin fish-hook, and tape fish-line.

The grandeur of the burning forest surpassed description. An immense sheet of flame, following to their tops the lofty trees of an almost impenetrable pine forest, leaping madly from top to top, and sending thousands of forked tongues a hundred feet or more athwart the midnight darkness, lighting up with lurid gloom and glare the surrounding scenery of lake and mountains, fills the beholder with mingled feelings of awe and astonishment. I never before saw anything so terribly beautiful. It was marvelous to witness the flash-like rapidity with which the flames would mount the loftiest trees. The roaring, cracking, crashing, and snapping of falling limbs and burning foliage was deafening. On, on, on traveled the destructive element, until it seemed as if the whole forest was enveloped in flame. Afar up the wood-crowned hill, the overtopping trees shot forth pinnacles and walls and streamers of arrowy fire. The entire hillside was an ocean of glowing and surging fiery billows.

Resolved to search for a trail no longer, when daylight came I selected for a landmark the lowest notch in the Madison Range. Carefully surveying the jagged and broken surface over which I must travel to reach it, I left the lake and pushed into the midst of its in-

tricacies. All the day, until nearly sunset, I struggled over rugged hills, through windfalls, thickets, and matted forests, with the rock-ribbed beacon constantly in view. As I advanced it receded, as if in mockery of my toil. Night overtook me with my journey half accomplished. The precaution of obtaining fire gave me warmth, and long before daylight I was on my way. The hope of finding an easy passage into the valley of the Madison inspired me with fresh courage and determination; but long before I arrived at the base of the range, I scanned hopelessly its insurmountable difficulties. It presented to my eager vision an endless succession of inaccessible peaks and precipices, rising thousands of feet sheer and bare above the plain. What a feeling of helpless despair came over me with the conviction that the journey of the last two days had been in vain! I seated myself on a rock, upon the summit of a commanding hill, and cast my eyes along the only route which now seemed tenable-down the Yellowstone. . . .

While I was considering whether to remain and search for a passage or return to the Yellowstone, I experienced one of those strange hallucinations which many of my friends have misnamed insanity, but which to me was Providence. An old clerical friend, for whose character and counsel I had always cherished peculiar regard, in some unaccountable manner seemed to be standing before me, charged with advice which would relieve my perplexity. I seemed to hear him say, as if in a voice and with the manner of authority:

"Go back immediately, as rapidly as your strength will permit. There is no food here, and the idea of scaling these rocks is madness."

30

31

30. *"Watching the sudden eruption of a geyser in famous Yellowstone", 1907.*

31. *Black Growler Geyser, circa 1904.*

32. *"Old Faithful" Geyser in eruption, 1904.*

32

33

33. A uniformed park guide (note the
    sidearm for defense against bears)
    explains geyser eruption to a tourist,
    circa 1903.

34. Geyser along the Firehole River, circa
    1903.

35. Comet Geyser, 1897.

36. A morning walk among the geysers, 1903.

34

35

36

37

37. "The new Grand Canyon Hotel", circa 1905.

38. The terraces and Mammoth Hot Springs Hotel, 1898.

39. 1903 tourist accomodations in Yellowstone.

38

39

"Doctor," I rejoined, "the distance is too great. I cannot live to travel it."

"Say not so. Your life depends upon the effort. Return at once. Start now, lest your resolution falter. Travel as fast and as far as possible-it is your only chance."

"Doctor, I am rejoiced to meet you in this hour of distress, but doubt the wisdom of your counsel. I am within seventy miles of Virginia. Just over these rocks, a few miles away, I will find my friends. My shoes are nearly worn out, my clothes are in tatters, and my strength is nearly overcome. As a last trial, it seems to me I can but attempt to scale this mountain or perish in the effort, if God so wills."

"Don't think of it. Your power of endurance will carry you through. I will accompany you. Put your trust in Heaven. Help yourself and God will help you."

DOANE: *Thirty-fourth day-September 24-*I arrived at Fort Ellis in the afternoon; distance 35 1/2 miles. Privates Moore and Williamson returned on the 2nd of October. They had gone back on the trail to our second camp, on the south side of the lake; thence struck the head of Snake River and followed down the stream for a distance of twenty-five miles from the Yellowstone Lake. They found game plentiful and tame, and had no difficulty in obtaining an abundant supply. After an ineffectual search of five days they followed our trail, arriving without incident at the above date.

EVERTS: I lost all sense of time. Days and nights came and went, and were numbered only by the growing consciousness that I was gradually starving. I felt no hunger, did not eat to appease appetite, but to renew strength. I experienced but little pain. The gaping sores on my feet, the severe burn on my hip, the festering crevices at the joints of my fingers, all terrible in appearance, had ceased to give me the least concern. The roots which supplied my food had suspended the digestive power of the stomach, and their fibres were packed in it in a matted compact mass.

Not so with my hours of slumber. They were visited by the most luxurious dreams. I would apparently visit the most gorgeous decorated restaurants of New York and Washington; sit down to immense tables spread with the most appetizing viands; partake of the richest oyster stews and plumpest pies; engage myself in the labor and preparation of curious dishes, and with them fill range upon range of elegantly furnished tables until they fairly groaned beneath the accumulated dainties prepared by my own hands....

It was a cold, gloomy day when I arrived in the vicinity of the falls. The sky was overcast and the snow-capped peaks rose chilly and bleak through the biting atmosphere. The moaning of the wind through the pines, mingling with the sullen roar of the falls, was strangely in unison with my own saddened feelings. I had no heart to gaze upon a scene which a few weeks before had inspired me with rapture and awe. One moment of sunshine was of more value to me than all the marvels amid which I was famishing. But the sun had hid his face and denied me all hope of obtaining fire....The coldness increased through the night. Constant friction with my hands and unceasing beating with my legs and feet saved me from freezing. It was the most terrible night of my journey, and when, with the early dawn, I pulled myself into a standing posture, it was to realize that my right arm was partially paralyzed, and my limbs so stiffened with cold as to be almost immovable. Fearing lest paralysis should suddenly seize upon the entire system, I literally dragged myself through the forest to the river. Seated near the verge of the great canyon below the falls, I anxiously awaited the appearance of the sun. That great luminary never looked so beautiful as when, a few moments afterward, he emerged from the clouds and exposed his glowing beams to the concentrated powers of my lens. I kindled a mighty flame, fed it with every dry stick and broken tree-top I could find, and without motion, and almost without sense, remained beside it several hours. The great falls of the Yellowstone were roaring within three hundred yards, and the awful canyon yawned almost at my feet; but they had lost all charm for me. In fact, I regarded them as enemies which had lured me to destruction, and felt a sullen satisfaction in morbid indifference.

My old friend and adviser, whose presence I had felt more than seen the last few days, now forsook me altogether. But I was not alone. By some process which I was too weak to solve, my arms, legs, and stomach were transformed into so many traveling companions. Often for hours I would plod along conversing with these imaginary friends. Each had his peculiar wants which he expected me to supply. The stomach was importunate in his demand for a change of diet-complained incessantly of the roots I fed him. I would try to silence him with promises, beg him to wait a few days, and when this failed of the quiet I desired, I would seek to intimidate him by declaring, as a sure result of negligence, our inability to reach home alive. All to no purpose-he tormented me with his fretful humors through the entire journey. The others would generally concur with him in these fancied altercations. The legs implored me for rest, and the arms complained that I gave them too much to do. Troublesome as they were, it was a pleasure to realize their presence. I worked for them, too, with right good will, doing many things for their seeming comfort which, had I felt myself alone, would have remained undone. They appeared to be perfectly helpless of themselves; would do nothing for me or for each other. I often wondered, while they ate and slept so much, that they did not aid in gathering wood and kindling fires. As a counterpoise to their own inertia, whenever they discovered languor in me, they were not waiting in words of encouragement and cheer. I recall an instance where, by prompt and timely interposition, the representative of the stomach saved me from a death of dreadful agony. One day I came to a small stream issuing from a spring of mild temperature on the hillside, swarming with minnows. I caught some

BY GIFFORD FOR NORTHERN PACIFIC RY. CO.

40

40. & 41. *1905 views of the Yellowstone River.*

41

42. *Tourist buggies along Gardiner River rapids, circa 1905.*

42

have clasped them from wrist to shoulder. "Yet," thought I, "it is death to remain; I cannot perish in this wilderness."

Taking counsel of this early formed resolution, I hobbled on my course through the snow, which was rapidly disappearing before the rays of the warm sun. Well knowing that I should find no thistles in the open country, I had filled my pouches with them before leaving the forest. My supply was running low, and there were yet several days of heavy mountain travel between me and Boteler's ranch.

Two or three days before I was found, while ascending a steep hill, I fell from exhaustion into the sage brush, without the power to rise. Unbuckling my belt, as was my custom, I soon fell asleep. I have no idea of the time I slept, but upon awaking I fastened my belt, scrambled to my feet, and pursued my journey. As night drew on I selected a camping-place, gathered wood into a heap, and felt for my lens to procure fire. It was gone. If the earth had yawned to swallow me I would not have been more terrified. The last hope had fled. I seemed to feel the grim messenger who had been so long pursuing me knocking at the portals of my heart as I lay down by the side of the wood-pile, and covered myself with limbs and sage brush, with the dreadful conviction that my struggle for life was over.

As calmness returned, reason resumed her empire. Fortunately, the weather was comfortable. I summoned all the powers of my memory, thought over every foot of the day's travel, and concluded that the glass must have become detached from my belt while sleeping. Five long miles over the hills must be retraced to regain it. There was no alternative, and before daylight I had staggered over half the distance. I found the lens on the spot where I had slept. No incident of my journey brought with it more of joy and relief.

Returning to the camp of the previous night, I lighted the pile I had prepared, and lay down for a night of rest. It was very cold, and towards morning commenced snowing. With difficulty I kept the fire alive. Sleep was impossible. When daylight came, I was impressed with the idea that I must go on despite the storm. Snatching a lighted brand, I started through the storm. In the afternoon the storm abated and the sun shone at intervals. Coming to a small clump of trees, I set to work to prepare camp. I laid the brand down which I had preserved with so much care, to pick up a few dry sticks with which to feed it, until I could collect wood for a camp-fire, and in the few minutes thus employed it expired. I sought to revive it, but every spark was gone. Clouds obscured the sun, now near the horizon, and the prospect of another night of exposure without fire became fearfully imminent. I sat down with my lens and the last remaining piece of touchwood I possessed to catch a gleam of sunshine, feeling that my life depended on it. In a few moments the cloud passed, and with trembling hands I presented the little disk to the face of the glowing luminary. Quivering with excitement lest a sudden cloud should interpose, a mo-

with my hands and ate them raw. To my taste they were delicious. But the stomach refused them, accused me of attempting to poison him, and would not be reconciled until I had emptied my pouch of the few fish I had put there for future use. Those that I ate made me very sick. Poisoned by the mineral in the water, had I glutted my appetite with them as I intended, I should doubtless have died in the wilderness, in excruciating torment.

At many of the streams on my route I spent hours in endeavoring to catch trout, with a hook fashioned from the rim of my broken spectacles, but in no instance with success. The tackle was defective. The country was full of game in great variety. I saw large herds of deer, elk, antelope, occasionally a bear, and many smaller animals. Numerous flocks of ducks, geese, swans, and pelicans inhabited the lakes and rivers. But with no means of killing them, their presence was a perpetual aggravation. . . .

Soon after leaving "Tower Falls," I entered the open country. Pine forests and windfalls were changed for sage brush and desolation, with occasional tracts of stinted verdure, barren hillsides, exhibiting here and there an isolated clump of dwarf trees, and ravines filled with the rocky debris of adjacent mountains. My first camp on this part of the route, for the convenience of getting wood, was made near the summit of a range of towering foot-hills. Towards morning a storm of wind and snow nearly extinguished my fire. I became very cold; the storm was still raging when I arose, and the ground white with snow. I was perfectly bewildered, and had lost my course of travel. No visible object, seen through the almost blinding storm, reassured me, and there was no alternative but to find the river and take my direction from the current. Fortunately, after a few hours of stumbling and scrambling among rocks and over crests, I came to the precipitous side of the canyon through which it ran, and with much labor, both of hands and feet, descended it to the margin. I drank copiously of its pure waters, and sat beside it for a long time, waiting for the storm to abate, so that I could procure fire. The day wore on, without any prospect of a termination to the storm. Chilled through, my tattered clothing saturated, I saw before me a night of horrors unless I returned to my fire. The scramble up the side of the rocky canyon, in many places nearly perpendicular, was the hardest work of my journey. Often while clinging to the jutting rocks with hands and feet, to reach a shelving protection, my grasp would unclose and I would slide many feet down the sharp declivity. It was night when, sore from the bruises I had received, I reached my fire; the storm, still raging, had nearly extinguished it. I found a few embers in the ashes, and with much difficulty kindled a flame. Here, on this bleak mountain side, as well as I now remember, I must have passed two nights beside the fire, in the storm. I remember, before I left this camp, stripping up my sleeves to look at my shrunken arms. The skin clung to the bones like wet parchment. A child's hand could ment passed before I could hold the lens steadily enough to concentrate a burning focus. At length it came. The little thread of smoke curled gracefully upwards from the Heaven-lighted spark, which a few moments afterwards, diffused with warmth and comfort my desolate lodgings.

I resumed my journey the next morning, with the belief that I should make no more fires with my lens. I must save a brand, or perish. The day was raw and gusty; and east wind, charge with storm, penetrated my nerves with irritating keenness. After walking a few miles the storm came on, and a coldness unlike any other I had ever felt seized me. It entered all my bones. I attempted to build a fire, but could not make it burn. Seizing a brand, I stumbled blindly on, stopping within the shadow of every rock and clump to renew energy for a final conflict for life. A solemn conviction that death was near, that at each pause I made my limbs would refuse further service, and that I should sink helpless and dying in my path, overwhelmed me with terror. Amid all this tumult of the mind, I felt that I had done all that man could do. Once only the thought flashed across my mind that I should be saved, and I seemed to hear a whispered command to "Struggle on." Groping along the side of a hill, I became suddenly sensible of a sharp reflection, as of burnished steel. Looking up, through half-closed eyes, two rough but kindly faces met my gaze.

"Are you Mr. Everts?"

"Yes, all that is left of him."

"We have come for you."

DOANE: Mr. Everts was found on the 10th of October by two men from the Yellowstone agency. On the first day of his absence he had left his horse standing unfastened, with all his arms and equipments strapped upon his saddle; the animal became frightened, ran away into the woods, and he was left without even a pocket-knife as a means of defense. Being very near-sighted, and totally unused to traveling in a wild country without guides, he became completely bewildered. He wandered down to the Snake River Lake, where he remained for twelve days, sleeping near the hot springs to keep from freezing at night, and climbing to the summits each day in the endeavor to trace out his proper course. Here he subsisted upon thistle-roots, boiled in the springs, and was kept up a tree the greater part of one night by a California lion. After gathering and cooking a supply of thistle-roots he managed to strike the southwest point of the lake, and followed around the north side to the Yellowstone, finally reaching our camp opposite the Grand Canon. He was twelve days out before he thought to kindle a fire by using the lenses of his field-glass, but afterward carried a burning brand with him in all his wanderings. Herds of game passed him during the night, on many occasions when he was on the verge of starvation. In addition to a tolerable supply of thistle-roots, he had nothing over thirty days but a handful of minnows and a couple of snow-birds. Twice he went five days without food, and three days without water, in that country which is a network of streams and springs. He was found on the verge of the great plateau, above the mouth of Gardiner's River. A heavy snow-storm had extinguished his fire; his supply of thistle-roots was exhausted; he was partially deranged, and perishing with cold. A large lion was killed near him, on the trail, which he said had followed him at a short distance for several days previously. It was a miraculous escape, considering the utter helplessness of the man.

43

44

43. *Hamming it upon the Pulpit Terrace formation, 1904.*

44. *Minerva Terrace with Hot Springs Hotel in background, 1904.*

45

45. *President Roosevelt (left) poses before*
    Liberty Cap during his 1903 western tour.

46. *Liberty Cap.*

46

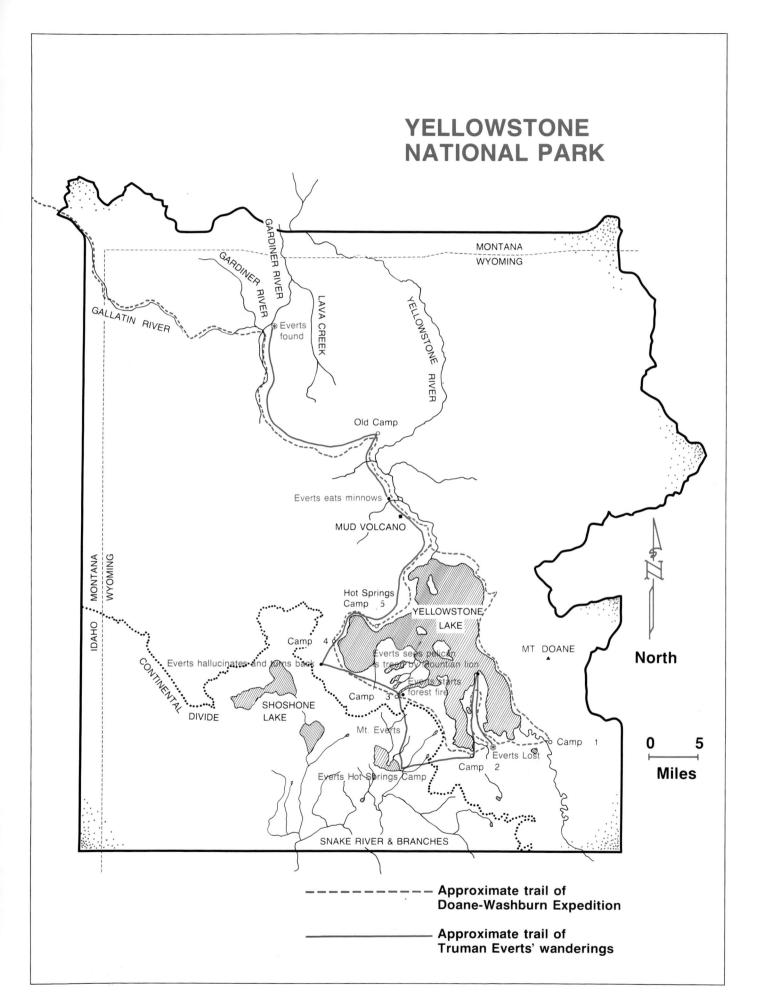

YELLOWSTONE NATIONAL PARK

MONTANA
WYOMING

GALLATIN RIVER

GARDINER RIVER

GARDINER RIVER

LAVA CREEK

YELLOWSTONE RIVER

⊛ Everts found

Old Camp

Everts eats minnows

MUD VOLCANO

Hot Springs
Camp 5

YELLOWSTONE
LAKE

MT DOANE

Camp 4

Everts hallucinates and turns back

Everts sees pelican
is treed by mountain lion

Everts starts
forest fire

Camp 3

SHOSHONE
LAKE

Mt. Everts

Camp 1

⊛ Everts Lost

Camp 2

Everts Hot Springs Camp

IDAHO
MONTANA
WYOMING

CONTINENTAL
DIVIDE

SNAKE RIVER & BRANCHES

North

0   5
Miles

– – – – – – – – – **Approximate trail of
Doane-Washburn Expedition**

————————— **Approximate trail of
Truman Everts' wanderings**

99

47

48

47, 48, & 49 Upright and prostrate petrified trunks along specimen ridge.

50. Touring the Yellowstone could be as luxurious or rugged as one chose. Sightseeing the Hoodoos by motorcar.

49

51

52

*51. & 52. Well-equipped and provisioned guides
lead anglers to great trout fishing by pack train.*

Yosemite National Park
P.O. Box 577
Yosemite National Park,
California 95389

National Park Service
Western
Regional Office
450 Golden Gate Avenue
Box 36063
San Francisco, California 94102
415/556-4122

YOSEMITE
NATIONAL PARK

53

54

55

53. The famed "Wawona Tree", standing 277 feet tall with a 26 foot diameter, was a favorite among motorized tourists.

54. "Room in the old Hutchings House - first in the valley - built around an 8 foot Cedar Tree", 1902.

55. The Wawona Tree amidst the Mariposa Grove, circa 1904.

56. Following spread: Huge redwood logs being trained from forest to mill, circa 1897.

Photographers delighted in celebrating Yosemite's wondrous heights:

57. "Overlooking nature's grandest scenery, Yosemite Valley, 1901.

58. Ranger posting fire lookout, circa 1905.

59. A perilous pose atop Glacier Point, 3,201 feet high.

57

58

59

60

61

60. *Another view of the oft-photographed Glacier Point, this one dramatically captioned, "Nearly a mile straight down and only a step", 1901.*

61. *From Clouds Rest (SE) over little Yosemite Valley to Mt. Clark (11,250 ft.), Sierra Nevada Mountains," 1902.*

62

62. "Mirror Lake, where nature multiplies her charms — looking (NE) to Mt. Watkins", 1902.

63. "Amidst Yosemite's charms - Sentinel Hotel, looking north across Valley to Yosemite Falls", 1902.

64. Amidst the majestic Heights and Chasms of wonderful Yosemite Valley - from Trail (NNW) to North and Basket Domes", 1902.

63

65

65. *Riders view Yosemite Falls from Glacier Point Trail, 1901.*

66. *"Enchanting view of wind-sprayed Yosemite Falls", circa 1902.*

Listing Of U.S. National Parks

67. John Burroughs and John Muir in the Yosemite Park, 1909.

LISTING OF U.S. NATIONAL PARKS

Alabama

Horseshoe Bend National Military Park, Route 1, Box 103, Daviston 36256

Russell Cave National Monument, Route 1, Box 175, Bridgeport 35740

Tuskegee Institute National Historic Site, P.O. Drawer 10, Tuskegee Institute 36088

Alaska

Aniakchak National Monument and Preserve, P.O. Box 7, King Salmon 99613

Bering Land Bridge National Preserve, P.O. Box 220, Nome 99762

Cape Krusenstern National Monument, P.O. Box 287, Kotzebue 99752

Denali National Park and Preserve, P.O. Box 9, Denali National Park 99755

Gates of the Arctic National Park and Preserve, Box 74680, Fairbanks 99707

Glacier Bay National Park and Preserve, Gustavus 99826

Katamai National Park and Preserve, P.O. Box 7, King Salmon 99613

Kenai Fjords National Park, P.O. Box 1727 Seward 99664

Klondike Gold Rush National Historical Park, P.O. Box 517, Skagway 99840

Kobuk Valley National Park, P.O. Box 287, Kotzebue 99752

Lake Clark National Pk. and Pre., 701 C. St., Box 61, Anchorage 99513

Noatak National Preserve, P.O. Box 287, Kotzebue 99752

Sitka National Historical Park, P.O. Box 738, Sitka 99835

Wrangell-St. Elias National Park and Preserve, P.O. Box 29, Glennallen 99588

Yukon-Charley Rivers National Preserve, P.O. Box 64, Eagle 99738

Arizona

Canyon de Chelly National Monument, P.O. Box 588, Chinle 86503

Casa Grande National Monument, P.O. Box 518, Coolidge 85228

Chiricahua National Monument, Dos Cabezas Route, Box 6500, Wilcox 85643

Coronado National Mem., R.R. 1 Box 126, Hereford 85615

Fort Bowie National Historic Site, P.O. 158, Bowie 85605

Grand Canyon National Park, P.O. Box 129, Grand Canyon 86023

Hubbell Trading Post National Historic Site, P. O. Box 150, Ganado 86505

Montezuma Castle National Monument, P.O. Box 219, Camp Verde 86322

Navajo National Monument, HC63, Box 3, Tonalea 86044

Organ Pipe Cactus National Monument, Route 1, Box 100, Ajo 85321

Petrified Forest National Park, P.O. Box 217, Petrified Forest, National Park 86028

Pipe Spring National Monument, Moccasin 86022

Saguaro National Mon, Route 8, Box 695, Tucson 85730

Sunset Crater National Monument, Tuba Star Route, Flagstaff 86001

Tonto National Monument, P.O. Box 707, Roosevelt 85545

Tumacacori National Monument, P.O. Box 67, Tumacacori 85640

Tuzigoot National Monument, P.O. Box 68, Clarkdale 86324

Walnut Canyon National Monument, Route 1, Box 25, Flagstaff 86001

Wupatki National Monument, HC 33 Box 444A, Flagstaff 86001

Arkansas

Arkansas Post National Mem., Route 1 Box 16, Gillett 72055

Buffalo National River, P.O. Box 1173, Harrison 72601

Fort Smith National Historic Site, P.O. Box 1406, Fort Smith 72902

Hot Springs National Park, P.O. Box 1860, Hot Springs National Park 71901

Pea Ridge National Military Park, Pea Ridge 72751

California

Cabrillo National Monument, P.O. Box 6670, San Diego 92106

Channel Islands National Park, 1699 Anchors Way Drive, Ventura 93003

Death Valley National Monument, (Calif, Nev.), Death Valley 92328

Devils Postpile National Mon, c/o Sequoia and Kings Can. National Parks, Three Riv. 93271

Eugene O'Neill National Hist Site, c/o John Muir NHS, 4202 Alhambra Ave., Martinez 94553

Fort Point National Historic Site, P.O. Box 29333, Presidio of San Francisco 94129

Golden Gate National Recreation Area, Fort Mason Bldg. 201, San Francisco 94123

John Muir National Historic Site, 4202 Alhambra Ave., Martinez 94553

Joshua Tree National Monument, 74485 National Monument Dr., Twentynine Palms 92277

Kings Canyon National Park, Three Rivers 93271

Lassen Volcanic National Park, Mineral 96063

Lava Beds National Monument, P.O. Box 867, Tulelake 96134

Muir Woods National Monument, Mill Valley 94941

© BY GIFFORD FOR NORTHERN PACIFIC RY CO

California, continued

Pinnacles National Monument, Paicines 95043
Point Reyes National Seashore, Point Reyes 94956
Redwood National Park, 1111 2nd St., Crescent
   City 95531
Santa Monica National Recreation Area, 22900
   Ventura Blvd., Suite 140, Woodland Hills 91364
Sequoia National Park, Three Rivers 93271
Whiskeytown-Shasta-Trinity National Recreation
   Area, Box 188, Whiskeytown 96095
Yosemite National Park, P.O. Box 577, Yosemite
   National Park 95389

Colorado

Bent's Old Fort National His. Site, 35110 Hwy. 194
   East, LaJunta 81050-9523
Black Canyon of the Gunnison National Monument,
P.O. Box 1648, Montrose 81402
Colorado National Monument, Fruita 81521
Curecanti National Recreation Area, P.O. Box 1040,
   Gunnison 81230
Dinosaur National Monument, (Colo, Utah), P.O.
   Box 210 Dinosuar 81610
Florissant Fossil Beds National Monument, P.O. Box
   185, Florissant 80816
Great Sands Dunes National Monument,
   Mosca 81146
Hovensweep National Monument (Colo, Utah), c/o
   Mesa Verde National Park 81330
Mesa Verde National Park, Mesa Verde National
   Park 81330
Rocky Monument National Park, Estes
   Park 80517

District of Columbia

Constitution Gardens. c/o National Capital Regional
   National Park Service, 1100 Ohio Dr., SW 20242
Ford's Theatre National Historic Site, 511 10th St.,
   NW 20004
Frederick Douglas Home, 1411 W. St. SE 20020
Kennedy Center for the Performing Arts National
   Park Serv., 2700 F St. NW 20566
Lincoln Memorial c/o National Park Serv., 1100
   Ohio Dr., SW 20242
Lyndon B. Johnson Memorial Grove on the
   Potomac, c/o George Washington Memorial
   Parkway, Turk. Run Park McLean, 22101
National Capital Park, 1100 Ohio Dr. SW 20242
Washington Monument, c/o National Park Service,
   1100 Ohio Dr., SW 20242
White House, c/o National Park, Service 1100 Ohio
   Dr., SW 20242
Vietnam Veterans Mem., c/o National Capital
   Regional National Park Service, 1100 Ohio Dr.,
   SW 20242

LISTING OF U.S. NATIONAL PARKS

Florida

Big Cypress National Pre., Star Rt. Box 110,
Ochopee 33943

Biscayne National Park, P.O. Box 1369,
Homestead 33030

Canaveral National Seashore, P.O. Box 6447,
Titusville 32780

Castillo de San Marcos National Mon, 1 Castillo
Drive, St. Augustine 32084

DeSoto National Memorial, 75th St., NW,
Bradenton 33529

Everglades National Park, P.O. Box 279,
Homestead 33030

Fort Caroline National Memorial, 12713 Fort Caroline
Road, Jacksonville 32225

Fort Jefferson National Monument, c/o U.S. Coast
Guard Base, Key West 33040

Gulf Island National Seashore, P.O. Box 100, Gulf
Breeze 32561 *(See also Miss.)*

Georgia

Andersonville National Historic Site,
Andersonville 31711

Chattahoochee National Area, 1900 Northridge
Road, Dunwoody 30338

Chickamauga & Chattanooga National Mil. Pk. Box
2128, Fort Oglethorpe 30742

Cumberland Island National Seashore, P.O. Box
806, St. Marys 31558

Fort Frederica National Monument, Route 4, Box
286C, St. Simons Island 31522

Fort Pulaski National Monument, P.O. Box 98,
Tybee Island 31328

Kennesaw Monument National Battlefield Park,
P.O. Box 1167, Marietta 30061

Martin Luther King, Jr., National Historic Site,
522 Auburn Ave, NE Atlanta 30312

Ocmulgee National Monument 1207 Emery
Highway, Macon 31201

Guam

War in the Pacific National Historic Parkway, Box
FA, Marine Dr. Asan, Agana 96910

Hawaii

Haleakala National Park, P.O. Box 369, Makawao,
Maui 96768

Hawaii Volcanoes National Park, Hawaii National
Park 96718

Pu'uhonua o Honaunau National Historic Park,
Box 128, Honaunau, Kona 96726

USS Arizona Memorial, 1 Arizona Memorial Place,
Honolulu 96818

USS Arizona Memorial, c/o Pacific Area Office, Box
50165, Honolulu 96850

Idaho

Craters of the Moon National Monument, P.O. Box
29, Arco 83213

Nez Perce National Historic Park, P.O. Box 93,
Spalding 83511

Illinois

Lincoln Home National Historic Site, 426 S. 7th
Street, Springfield 62703

Indiana

George Rogers Clark National Historic Park 401 S.
2nd Street, Vincennes 47591

IN Dunes National Lakeshore, 1100 N. Mineral
Springs, Road, Porter 46304

Lincoln Boyhood National Memorial, Lincoln
City 47552

Iowa

Effigy Mounds National Monument, P.O. Box K.,
McGregor 52157

Herbert Hoover National Historic Site, Old Fort
Boulevard, Fort Scott 66701

Kansas

Fort Larned National Historic Site, Route 3,
Larned 67550

Fort Scott National Historic Site, Old Fort
Boulevard, Fort Scott 66701

Kentucky

Abraham Lincoln Birthplace National Historic Site,
R.F.D. 1, Hodgenville 42748

Cumberland Gap Historic Park (KY, TN, VA), P.O.
Box 840, Middlesboro 40965

Mammoth Cave National Park, Mammoth Cave 42259

Louisiana

J. Lafitte National Historic Park & Preserve, c/o US
Customs House, 423 Canal St., Rm. 206, New
Orleans 70130

Maine

Acadia National Park, P.O. Box 177, Bar
Harbor 04609

Maryland

Antietam National Battlefield Site, Box 158,
Sharpsburg 21782

Assateague Island National Seashore (MD., VA.),
Route 2, Box 294, Berlin 21811

Catoctin Monument Park, Thurmont 21788

Chesapeake & OH Canal National Historic Park, Box
158, Sharpsburg 21782

Clara Barton National Historic Site, 5801 Oxford
Road, Glen Echo 20768

Fort McHenry National Monument & Historic
Shrine, E. Fort Avenue, Baltimore 21230

Fort WA Park, Capital Parks - E., 1900 Anacostia
Drive SE 20019

Greenbelt Park, 6501 Greenbelt Road,
Greenbelt 20770
Hampton National Historic Site, 5354 Hampton
Lane, Towson 21240
Piscataway Park, National Cap. Parks East, 1900
Anacostia Dr. SE 20019

Massachusetts
Adams National Historic Site, 135 Adams Street,
Box 531, Quincy 02269
Boston National Historic Park, Charlestown Navy
Yard, Boston 02129
Cape Cod National Seashore, South Wellfleet 02663
Frederick Law Olmsted National Historic Site, 99
Warren St., Brookline 02146
John Fitzgerald Kennedy National Historic Site, 83
Beals Street Brookline 02146
Longfellow National Historic Site, 105 Brattle
Street, Cambridge 02138
Lowell National Historic Park, P.O. Box 1098,
Lowell 10853
Minute Man National Historic Park, Box 160,
174 Liberty Street, Concord 01742
Salem Maritime National Historic Site, Custom
House, Derby Street, Salem 01970
Sangus Iron Works National Historic Site, 244
Central Street, Saugus 01906
Springfield Armory National Historic Site, 1 Armory
Square, Springfield 01105

Michigan
Isle Royale National Park, 87 N. Ripley Street,
Houghton 49931
Pictured Rocks National Lakeshore, P.O. Box 40,
Munising 49862
Sleeping Bear Dunes National Lakeshore, 400 Main
Street, Frankfort 49635

Minnesota
Grand Portage National Monument, P.O. Box 666,
Grand Marais 55604
Pipestone National Monument, Box 727,
Pipestone 56164
Voyageurs National Park, Box 50, International
Falls 56649

Mississippi
Brices Cross Roads National Battlefield Site,
c/o Natchez Trace Parkway, R.R. 1, NT-143,
Tupelo 38801
Gulf Islands National Seashore, 3500 Park Road,
Ocean Springs 39564
Natchez Trace Parkway (MS, AL, TN), R.R. 1,
NT-143, Tupelo 38801
Tupelo Battlefield, c/o Natchez Trace Pkwy., R.R. 1,
NT-143, Tupelo 38801

Mississippi continued

Vicksburg National Nil. Park, 3201 Clay Street,
  Vicksburg 39180

Missouri

George Washington Carver National Monument,
  P.O. Box 38, Diamond 64840
Harry S. Truman National Historic Site, P.O. Box
  4139, Independence 64075
Jefferson National Exp. Mememorial National
  Historic Site, 11 N. 4th St. St. Louis 63102
Ozark National Scenic Riverways, P.O. Box 490,
  Van Buren 63965
Wilson's Creek National Battlefield, Postal Drawer
  C, Republic 65738

Montana

Big Hole National Battlefield, P.O. Box 237,
  Wisdom 59761-0237
Bighorn Can. National Recreation Area (MT, WY).,
  P.O. Box 458, Fort Smith 59035
Custer Battlefield National Monument, P.O. Box 39,
  Crow Agency 59022
Glacier National Park, W. Glacier 59936
Grant-Kohrs Ranch National Historic Site, P.O.
  Box 790, Deer Lodge 59722

Nebraska

Agate Fossil Beds National Monument, P.O. Box
  427, Gering 69341
Homestead National Monument of America, Route
  3, Box 47, Beatrice 68310-9416
Scotts Bluff National Monument, P.O. Box 427,
  Gering 69341

Nevada

Lake Mead National Recreation Area (NV, AZ),
  601 Nevada Highway, Boulder City 89005
Lehman Caves National Monument, Baker 89311

New Hampshire

St.-Gaudens National Historic Site, R.R. 2,
  Box 73, Cornish 03745

New Jersey

Edison National Historic Site, Main St. & Lakeside
  Avenue, W. Orange 07052
Gateway National Recreation Area (Saney Hook
  Unit), Box 437, Highlands 07732
Morristown National Historic Park, Washington
  Place, Morristown 07960

New Mexico

Aztec Ruins National Monument, P.O. Box U,
Aztec 87410

Bandelier National Monument, Los Alamos 87544

Capulin Monument National Monument,
Capulin 88414

Carlsbad Caverns National Park, 3225 National
Parks Highway, Carlsbad 88220

Chaco Culture National Historic Park, Star Route 4,
Box 6500, Bloomfield 87413

El Morro National Monument, Ramah 87321

Fort Union National Monument, Watrous 87753

Gila Cliff Dwellings, Gila Hot Springs, Route 11,
Box 100, Silver City 88061

Pecos National Monument, P.O. Drawer 11,
Pecos 87552

Salinas National Monument, P.O. Box 496,
Mountainair 87036

White Sands National Monument, P.O. Box 458,
Alamogordo 88310

New York

Castle Clinton National Monument, c/o Manhattan
Sites, NPS, 26 Wall Street, N.Y. 10005

E. Roosevelt National Historic Site, 249 Albany Post
Road, Hyde Park 12538

Federal Hall National Memorial, c/o Manhattan
Sites, NPS, 26 Wall St., N.Y. 10005

Fire Island National Seashore, 120 Laurel Street,
Patchogue 11772

Fort Stanwix National Monument, 112 E. Park
Street, Rome 13440

Gateway National Recreation Area, Floyd Bennett
Field, Building 69 Brooklyn 11234

General Grant National Memorial, Manhattan Sites
National Park Service, 26 Wall St., NY 10005

Hamilton Grange National Memorial, 287 Convent
Avenue, N.Y. 10031

Home of F.D. Roosevelt National Historic Site, 249
Albany Post Road, Hyde Park 12538

Martin Van Buren National Historic Site, P.O. Box
545, Kinderhook 12106

Sagamore Hill National Historic Site, Cove Neck
Road, #304, Oyster Bay 11771

Saratoga National Historic Park, R.D. 2, Box 33,
Stillwater 12170

Statue of Liberty National Monument, (N.Y., N.J.),
Liberty Island, N.Y. 10004

T. Roosevelt Birthplace National Historic Site,
28 E. 20th St., N.Y. 10003

T. Roosevelt Inaugural National Historic Site, 641
Delaware Avenue, Buffalo 14202

Vanderbilt Mansion National Historic Site, 249
Albany Post Road, Hyde Park 12538

Women's Rights National Historic Park, 116 Fall
Street, P.O. Box 70, Seneca Falls 13148

North Carolina

Blue Ridge Parkway (NC, VA.), 700 NW Bank
Building, Asheville 28801

Cape Hatteras National Seashore, Route 1, Box 675,
Manteo 27954

Cape Lookout National Seashore, P.O. Box 690,
Beaufort 28516

C. Sandburg Home National Historic Site, P.O.
Box 395, Flat Rock 28731

Fort Raleigh National Historic Site, Cape Hatteras
Gp., Route 1, Box 675, Manteo 27954

Guilford Courthouse National Mil. Park, P.O. Box
9806, Greensboro 27408

Moores Creek National Battlefield, P.O. Box 69,
Currie 28435

Wright Brothers National Memorial, Cape Hatteras
Gp., Rt. 1, Box 675, Manteo 27954

North Dakota

Fort Union Trading Post National Historic Site,
Buford Route, Williston 58801

Knife River Indian Village National Historic Site,
R.R. 1, Stanton 58571

Theodore Roosevelt National Park, P.O. Box 7,
Medora 58645

Ohio

Cuyahoga Valley National Recreation Area, 15610
Vaughn Road, Brecksville 44141

James A. Garfield National Historic Site, Lawnfield,
1950 Mentor Ave., Mentor 44060

Mound City Group National Monument, 16062
Street, Route 104, Chillicothe 45601

Perry's Victory and International Peace Memorial,
P.O. Box 549, Put-in-Bay 43456

William H. Taft. National Historic Site, 2038
Auburn Avenue, Cincinnati 45219

Oklahoma

Chickasaw National Recreation Area, P.O. Box 201,
Sulphur 73086

Oregon

Crater Lake National Park, P.O. Box 7,
Crater Lake 97604

Fort Clatsop National Memorial, Route 3, Box
604-FC, Astoria 97103

John Day Fossil Beds National Monument 420 W.
Main Street, John Day 97845

OR Caves National Monument, 19000 Caves
Highway, Cave Jct. 97523

Pennsylvania

Allegheny Portage Rail Road National Historic Site,
P.O. Box 247, Cresson 16630

DA Water Gap National Recreation Area (PA, N.J.),
Bushkill 18324

Edgar Allen Poe National Historic Site,
313 Walnut St., Philadelphia 19106

Fort Necessity National Battlefield, The National
Pike, R.D. 2, Box 528, Farmington 15437

Gettysburg National Mil. Park, Gettysburg 17325

Hopewell Village National Historic Site, R.D. 1,
Box 345, Elverson 19520

Independence National Historic Park, 313 Walnut
Street, Philadelphia 19106

Johnstown Flood National Memorial, c/o Allegheny
Portage Rail Road National Historic Site, P.O. Box
247, Cresson 16630

T. Kosciuszko National Memorial, c/o Independence
National Historic Park, 313 Walnut St.,
Philadelphia 19106

Upper Delaware Scenic & Recreation River
(PA, NY), P.O. Box C, Narrowsburg 12764

Valley Forge National Historic Park,
Valley Forge 19481

Puerto Rico

San Juan National Historic Site, P.O. Box 712
San Juan 00902

Rhode Island

Roger Williams National Memorial, P.O. Box 367
Annex Station, Providence 02901

South Carolina

Congaree Swamp National Monument, P.O.,
Box 11938, Columbia 29211

Cowpens National Battlefield, P.O.Box 308,
Chesnee 29323

Fort Sumter National Monument, 1214 Middle
Street, Sullivans Island 29482

Kings Mountain National Military Park, P.O.
Box 31, Kings Mountain 28086

Ninety Six National Historic Site, P.O. Box 496
Ninety Six 29666

South Dakota

Badlands National Park, P.O. Box 6, Interior 57760

Jewel Cave National Monument, P.O. Box 351,
Custer 57730

Mount Rushmore National Memorial, P.O. Box 268,
Keystone 57751

Wind Cave National Park, Hot Springs 57747

Tennessee

A Johnson National Historic Site, Col. & Depot Sts.
Greenville 57743

Big S. Fork National River & Recreation Area,
P.O. Drawer 630, Oneida 37841

Fort Donelson National Military Park, P.O. Box F,
Dover 37058

Great Smoky Mountains National Park (TN, NC),
Garlinburg 37738

Tennessee, continued

Obed Wild & Scenic River, P.O. Drawer 630,
Oneida 37841

Shiloh National Military Park, P.O. Box 61,
Shiloh 38376

Stones River National Battlefield, Route 10, Box 495
Murfreesboro 37130

Texas

Alibates Flint Quarries National Monument, c/o
Lake Meredith NRA, P.O. Box 1438, Fritch 79036

Amistad National Recreation Area, P.O. Box
420367, Del Rio 78842

Big Bend National Park, Big Bend National
Park 79834

Big Thicket National Preserve, P.O. Box 7408,
Beaumont 77706

Chamizal National Memorial, P.O. Box 722,
El Paso 79944-0722

Fort Davis National Historic Site, P.O. Box 1456,
Fort Davis 79734

Guadalupe Mountains National Historic Park, 3225
National Parks Highway, Carlsbad 88220

Lake Meredith National Recreation Area, P.O. Box
1438, Fritch 79036

Lyndon Baines Johnson National Historic Park,
P.O. Box 329, Johnson City 78636

Padre Island National Seashore, 9405 S.
Padre Island Drive, Corpus Christi 78418

San Antonio Missions National Historic Park, 727 E.
Durango, San Antonio 78206

Utah

Arches National Park, 446 S. Main Street,
Moab 84532

Bryce Canyon National Park, Bryce Canyon 84717

Canyonlands National Park, 446 S. Main St.,
Moab 84532

Capitol Reef National Park, Torrey 84775

Cedar Breaks National Monument, P.O. Box 749,
Cedar City 84720

Glen Canyon National Recreation Area (UT, AZ),
P.O. Box 1507, Page 86040

Golden Spike National Historic Site, P.O. Box W,
Brigham City 84302

Natural Bridges National Monument, c/o
Canyonlands National Park, 446 S. Main Street,
Moab 84532

Rainbow Bridge National Monument, c/o Glen
Canyon National Recreation Area, P.O. Box 1507,
Page 86040

Timpanogos Cave National Monument, R.R. 3, Box
200, American Fork 84003

Zion National Park, Springdale 84767-1099

LISTING OF U.S. NATIONAL PARKS

Virginia

Appomattox Court House National Historic Park, Box 218, Appomattox 24522

Arlington House, The Robert E. Lee Memorial, c/o George Washington Memorial Parkway, Turkey Run Park, McLean 22101

Booker T. Washington National Monument, Route 1 Box 195, Hardy 24101

Colonial National Historic Park, P.O. Box 210, Yorktown 23690

Fredericksburg & Spotsylvania Natl. Mil. Park, Box 679, Fredericksburg 22404

George Washington Birthplace National Monument, Washington's Birthplace 22575 G. Washington Memorial, Parkway (VA, MD), Turkey Run Park, McLean 22101

Maggie L. Walker National Historic Site, c/o Richmond National Battlefield Park, 3215 E. Broad Street, Richmond 23223

Manassas National Battlefield Park, P.O. Box 1830, Manassas 22110

Petersburg National Battlefield, P.O. Box 549, Petersburg 23834

Prince William Forest Park, P.O. Box 208, Triangle 22172

Richmond National Battlefield Park, 3215 E. Broad Street, Richmond 23223

Shenandoah National Park, Luray 22835

Wolf Trap Farm Park for the Performing Arts, 1551 Trap Rd., Vienna 22180

Virgin Islands

Buck Island Reef National Monument, Box 160, Christiansted, St. Croix 00820

Virgin Islands National Park, P.O. Box 7789, St. Thomas 00801

Washington

Coulee Dam National Recreation Area, P.O. Box 37, Coulee Dam 99116

Fort Vancouver National Historic Site, 1501 E. Evergreen Boulevard, Vancouver 98661-3897

Klondike Gold Rush National Historic Park, 117 S. Main St., Seattle 98104

Lake Chelan National Recreation Area, 800 State Street, Sedro Woolley 98284

Mount Rainier National Park, Tahoma Woods, Star Route, Ashford 98304

N. Cascades National Park, 800 State Street, Sedro Woolley 98284

Olympic National Park, 600 E. Park Avenue, Port Angeles 98362

Ross Lake National Recreation Area, 800 State Street, Sedro Woolley 98284

Washington, continued

San Juan Island National Historic Park, 300 Cattle Point Road, Friday Harbor 98250

Whitman Mission National Historic Site, R.R. 2, Box 247, Walla Walla 99362

West Virginia

Harpers Ferry National Historic Park, (WV, MD, VA), Box 65, Harpers Ferry 25425

New River Gorge National River, P.O. Drawer V, Oak Hill 25901

Wisconsin

Apostle Island National Lakeshore, P.O. Box 729, Bayfield 54814

St. Croix & Lower St. Croix National Scenic Riverway, (WI, MN), Box 708, St. Croix Falls 54024

Wyoming

Devils Tower National Monument, Devils Tower 82714

Fort Laramie National Historic Site, Fort Laramie 82212

Fossil Butte National Monument, P.O. Box 527, Kemmerer 83101

Grand Teton National Park, P.O. Box Drawer 170, Moose 83012

J. D. Rockefeller, Jr., Memorial Parkway, c/o Grand Teton National Park, P.O. Drawer 170, Moose 83012

Yellowstone National Park, P.O. Box 168, Yellowstone National Park 82190

Source: United States Department of Interior, National Park Service

For Further Reading

Albright, Horace M.,
The Birth of the National Park Service (as told to Robert Cahn). Howe, Salt Lake City, 1985.

Bartlett, Richard A.,
Yellowstone: A Wilderness Besieged, University of Arizona, Tucson 1985.

Everhart, William C.,
The National Park Service, Westview, Boulder, CO, 1983.

Frome, Michael,
The Future of the National Parks, University of Arizona, Tucson, 1991.
Strangers in High Places: The Story of the Great Smoky Mountains,
University of Tennessee, Knoxville, 1980.

Muir, John,
Our National Parks, University of Wisconsin, Madison, 1981 (first published 1901).

Runte, Alfred,
National Parks: The American Experience, University of Nebraska, 1987.
Yosemite, the Embattled Wilderness, University of Nebraska, 1990.

Sax, Joseph L.,
Mountains Without Handrails, University of Michigan, Ann Arbor, 1980.

Shankland, Robert,
Steve Mather of the National Parks, Alfred Knopf, New York, 1954.

Swain, Donald C.,
Wilderness Defender: Horace M. Albright and Conservation,
University ofChicago, 1970.

Wolfe, Linnie Marsh,
Son of the Wilderness: The Life of John Muir, University of Wisconsin,
Madison (first published in 1945).

About The Author

Michael Frome has been called "the conscience of the national parks" and "the voice of the wilderness" for all his writing and speaking over a period of forty years in their behalf. He has enjoyed a colorful and creative career, which he continues to pursue with enthusiasm and energy, exploring the great areas that he loves as backpacker, camper, canoer and horseman.

Born in New York City, he served as a World War II transport navigator, flying to distant corners of the world. Since then he has been a newspaper reporter, magazine writer and columnist, educator, and eloquent conservationist. He is now a member of the faculty of Huxley College of Environmental Studies at Western Washington University (Bellingham, Washington), pioneering a program in environmental journalism and writing. In 1981, he received an award from his colleagues in the American Society of Journalists and Authors for the Best Magazine Article of the Year (a series on the "The Un-Greening of the National Parks"). In 1986, he received the Marjory Stoneman Douglas Award from the National Parks and Conservation Association for his many years of work on behalf of national parks.

More than 500,000 copies of his *National Park Guide*, published for years by Rand McNally, more recently by Prentice Hall, have guided travelers to America's wonderlands. His most recent book is *Conscience of a Conservationist*, while his newest, *The Future of the National Parks*, is due for publication in 1991. Other books include *Strangers in High Places — The Story of the Great Smokey Mountains*; *Battle for the Wilderness*; and *Promised Land — Adventures and Encounters in Wild America*.

Senator Gaylord Nelson of Wisconsin declared in Congress: "No writer in America has more persistently and effectively argued for the need of national ethics of environmental stewardship than Michael Frome."